Critical Guides to French Texts

96 Pagnol: La Gloire de mon père *and* Le Château de ma mère

Critical Guides to French Texts

EDITED BY ROGER LITTLE, WOLFGANG VAN EMDEN, DAVID WILLIAMS

PAGNOL

La Gloire de mon père *and*
Le Château de ma mère

David Coward

Reader in French
University of Leeds

Grant & Cutler Ltd
1992

I.S.B.N. 84-599-3298-2

DEPÓSITO LEGAL: V. 3.589-1992

Printed in Spain by
Artes Gràficas Soler, S.A., Valencia
for
GRANT & CUTLER LTD
55-57 GREAT MARLBOROUGH STREET, LONDON W1V 2AY

Contents

Prefatory Note

Reference throughout is made to the most recent paperback editions of *La Gloire de mon père* and *Le Château de ma mère* which are published under the Fortunio imprint by the Editions de Fallois, details of which are given in the Bibliography. The first reference in a paragraph is specified as *Gloire* or *Château*, subsequent references within the paragraph being to that volume unless a change is indicated. Cross-references of the type (*13*, p.9) relate to the Bibliography at the end of this study.

1. Genesis and Genre

Marcel Pagnol became famous in 1928 with *Topaze*, the most successful of a series of plays satirising the moral corruption of French society in the aftermath of the Great War. In 1930, he abandoned the theatre after announcing that the new 'talking' pictures were the complete modern form of dramatic art. In the next ten years he made a dozen films, including the celebrated 'trilogie marseillaise', all set in the Midi and all enormously popular. By the end of the thirties, he was France's most successful independent film producer. During the German Occupation, he withdrew to the hills above Cagnes-sur-Mer and maintained a discreet silence. He was elected to the French Academy in 1946, the first *cinéaste* to be so honoured, and took his duties as an 'intellectual' seriously. He published his translation of *Hamlet* and a small treatise on comedy, *Notes sur le rire* (1947) and began turning Virgil into French verse. Dedicated to the memory of his brother Paul, 'le dernier chevrier de Virgile', *Les Bucoliques* appeared in 1957.

Meanwhile, he continued to write and direct films but never quite regained his popularity with the post-war public which preferred stronger meat to his soft-centred view of human nature. *Manon des sources* (1952) and an adaptation of Alphonse Daudet's *Lettres de mon moulin* (1954) were critical successes but did not do well enough at the box-office to encourage producers to invest in further ventures. Pagnol attempted a return to the theatre with *Judas* (1955) and *Fabien* (1956). When both failed, his stock fell several more points and he cast around for a new avenue to explore.

Pagnol, who had the pleasant habit of answering questions with a story, told a journalist friend how he discovered a new channel for his talents. When dining with friends in the autumn of 1956, he explained, he was asked by Hélène Lazareff, editor of *Elle* magazine, to write 'un petit conte avec une histoire du temps où j'étais gosse que je lui avais racontée et qui avait plu. D'abord, j'ai essayé de me dérober. Je lui dis que ce n'est pas mon métier d'écrire des romans ou des nouvelles, que je ne suis qu'un auteur dramatique, que je sais tout au plus faire parler les gens.' Out of politeness, however, he finally agreed and one day a messenger arrived on his doorstep claiming he would be dismissed if he did not return with at least part of the promised story. Feeling sorry for the man, Pagnol hurriedly wrote six pages.

> Et voilà qu'en écrivant, ça m'a intéressé. Tout à coup, j'ai revu mes parents. Je les ai revus avec cette impression curieuse d'être, moi, infiniment plus vieux qu'ils ne l'étaient à l'époque où je les faisais revivre. Par rapport à l'homme que j'étais devenu, c'étaient alors des enfants. Cette pensée m'a inspiré... (6, p.1)

This account of the genesis of the *Souvenirs d'enfance*, like most of the stories Pagnol told about himself, contains elements of truth beneath a thick coating of self-deprecating charm. Roger Richebé, an old friend, distinctly recalled that Pagnol had begun work on his autobiography some time before the invitation from *Elle*. Moreover, according to Pagnol's sister, Mme Germaine Gombert ('la petite soeur'), he had rented a house at La Treille in January 1956 and, armed with a Geiger counter, began prospecting on land he had acquired at various times. Pagnol, a keen dowser and amateur scientist, had heard that the Germans had discovered uranium in the area during the war. He found no uranium but instead, as he roamed through countryside which he had not explored since he was a boy, he uncovered a rich seam of memories. He was of an age to appreciate them, as he later told Marcel Mithois:

> ...en vieillissant on perd la mémoire, je veux dire qu'on perd la faculté d'enregistrer de nouveaux souvenirs mais on ne perd pas ses souvenirs. Au contraire, il semble qu'ils se précisent... il semble que le disque — c'est une

comparaison stupide — que le disque que nous avons
dans la tête lorsqu'on est jeune est très tendre. Tout s'y
inscrit magnifiquement, puis, à mesure qu'on vieillit, il
se durcit... alors on ne peut plus enregistrer aussi bien.
Mais ce qui a été inscrit dans la jeunesse ressort
fortement (...) Mes souvenirs d'enfance je ne les avais
pas pendant ma vie, je les avais à cinquante-cinq ans
(...); au moment où l'on commence à vieillir tout ça
remonte, tout ça revient avec une très grande facilité.
(*13*, p.9)

Evelyn Waugh once said that a writer turns to his past only when he
has lost interest in the future. Pagnol still had ambitions to fulfil —
he was then working on mathematical problems and a study of the
Man in the Iron Mask — and preferred a more gently self-
disparaging formula: 'A mon âge, je n'ai plus de mémoire, il ne me
reste que des souvenirs'. In a sense, it was a natural development to
dwell on the strongest of those memories: his *souvenirs d'enfance*.

But whatever the truth behind his much embellished tale of the
Lazareff dinner, where he had entertained the company with an
account of the 'quatre châteaux' which barred the way to La Treille,
segments of his childhood memories were duly serialised in *Elle* in
five weekly parts as *Le Château de ma mère* between December 3
and 31, 1956. A few prefatory comments, absent from the final
version, helped define the mood as playful and affectionate:

Ceci se passait vers 1905, et selon mes calculs de cette
époque, la famille avait soixante-treize ans: deux pour la
petite soeur, six pour mon frère Paul, neuf pour moi,
vingt-six pour ma mère et trente pour mon père, notre
patriarche. Il était alors maître d'école à Marseille et
nous l'admirions pour sa force, sa beauté, son adresse au
jeu de boules, son talent de flûtiste et surtout sa façon
désinvolte d'aiguiser son rasoir sur la paume de sa main
gauche...

The articles were an immediate success and, encouraged by the appreciative letters sent by readers and urged on by his friend, the publisher Clément Pastorelly, Pagnol produced enough material to fill two volumes. *La Gloire de mon père* appeared in November 1957 and *Le Château de ma mère* in April 1958.

Book distributors were at first sceptical about the commercial wisdom of his change of direction: would Pagnol's public, which knew him as a man of the theatre and the cinema, follow him into print? Pagnol shared their misgivings for the literary reasons which he sets out in the published preface to *La Gloire de mon père*. On the copy he sent to André Billy, he described himself as 'un débutant assez intimidé' and on another, sent to Pierre Rocher, he wrote: 'Voilà mon premier livre, et j'en suis tout effrayé' (7, p. 239). He may have overstated his fears as a way of pre-empting hostile criticism, but his caution seems to have been quite genuine: the first printing of *La Gloire de mon père* was limited to 3,000 copies, a figure only a little in excess of the print-run for any first novel and well below the 25,000 advance printing of a later title with an even more restricted appeal, *Le Masque de fer* (1964), in which, incidentally, he attributes Louis XIV's autocratic behaviour to his early training: 'Les impressions de l'enfance sont ineffaçables' (*Œuvres complètes*, X, pp.273-74).

Both the fears of the book-trade and Pagnol's uncertainties as a late-starting 'writer of prose' proved unfounded. Reviewers were charmed and saluted a new 'classic' of French literature. André Billy (*Le Figaro*, 8 January 1958) called *La Gloire de mon père* 'délicieux' and predicted that it would outlast the ever popular *Marius* and *Topaze*. Lucien Rebatet (*Rivarol*, 13 October 1960) was unstinting in his praise of *Le Château de ma mère*: 'Il n'y a que du soleil dans le livre de Pagnol'. When Rita Barisse's translation of both volumes (as *The Days were Too Short* (1960)) was reissued in 1962, S.H. Berhman warmed to Pagnol's qualities: 'his enormous gusto for life, his humor, sympathy and wit, his keen satiric sense and his inexorable eye for reality' (*New York Review of Books*, 23 October 1962). Only the *Times Literary Supplement* (23 December 1960) sounded a sour note: 'in no way an original writer', Pagnol indulges the picturesque and the sentimental in a 'boring' reminiscence which culminates in the 'tedious' shooting party and offers 'no particular insight into child psychology. He has little to say and says it rather badly, falling too often into unconvincing dialogue'.

The public did not share this view, and Pagnol quickly won over a new generation of young readers who proved as enthusiastic consumers of his 'prose' as their parents and grandparents had been of his plays and films. He received a considerable fan-mail from all age-groups. Georges Berni (7, p.240) quotes one letter from an eleven-year-old who wrote: 'Je préfère vos livres à ceux spécialement écrits pour les enfants car ce que vous dites est vrai, et je retrouve mes idées dans les vôtres'. But Pagnol was even more gratified to hear from a retired school-teacher who not only declared that 'votre livre est un chef-d'oeuvre' but added that 'il est plein de dictées' (9, p.167). Since 1977, both volumes have figured on the official secondary syllabus. Extracts appear in classroom anthologies and a number of school editions of both texts have appeared. As a 'mémorialiste', Pagnol had found a third career.

Encouraged by his success, he resolved to extend his autobiography to cover his school-days. His new 'trilogie' would be completed by a volume entitled *Les Grandes Amours* or *Les Belles Amours*. His typescript, however, was judged too long for one volume and not long enough for two. He agreed nevertheless to publish part of the text which he would complete in due course. *Le Temps des secrets* (1960), though judged to fall below the standard set by its predecessors, was nevertheless very well received. It tells how Marcel's hunting exploits with Lili are curtailed by his infatuation with Isabelle and how, in defeating the bully Pegomas, he acquires a personality at the Lycée where he begins to live a life of his own outside the influence of his family. Plans for a final instalment, to be called *Le Temps des amours*, were interrupted by other interests and commitments. His first novel, *L'Eau des collines* (comprising *Jean de Florette* and *Manon des sources*) appeared in 1963 as did the series of prefaces which he wrote for his *Œuvres complètes*, while the following year saw the publication of his study of *Le Masque de fer*. But he had not lost sight of his autobiography.

He considered the possibility of filming the first volumes and at one point thought of casting Geraldine Chaplin in the role of Augustine. At various times, he subsequently published a number of episodes from this fourth volume in *Paris-Match* and other magazines. His intentions were clear enough:

> C'est la suite de l'enfance. Ca s'arrête à l'âge de quatorze ans. Parce qu'il me semble qu'après on raconte sa vie personnelle, alors ça devient des confidences... Lorsqu'on parle d'un enfant qu'on a été mais qu'on n'est plus, c'est encore possible, mais il ne faut pas trop parler de sa vie privée. C'est pourquoi ce quatrième tome sera le dernier. (*13*, p.9)

He returned to the task on numerous occasions, recasting the volume and rewriting whole sections, as Bernard de Fallois explains (*Amours*, pp.247-73). But, though many begged him to continue the story, he hesitated. He had already removed the word *Amours* from the title of the third volume and was reluctant to embark upon the delicate problems of early adolescence:

> J'avais choisi le premier titre [i.e., *Le Temps des amours*, which he had changed to *Le Temps des secrets*] un peu à la légère. Sans que je l'aie cherché, je me suis aperçu très vite que, dès leur parution, les enfants étaient devenus les lecteurs privilégiés de mes deux premiers livres. C'étaient eux qui en avaient fait le succès. Je recevais des lettres d'écoliers, d'écolières, bouleversantes, de classes entières entassant au bas de la page les signatures de tous les élèves. J'ai pensé que c'était un public très pur, très chaste. Il m'a semblé que si je leur racontais l'éveil à la vie de mon héros, ses premiers émois sexuels, je risquais de les choquer. Je me suis imposé une censure. J'ai changé le sujet et le titre. (*11*, p.340)

It is difficult to say whether it was for such scruples (which did not, however, extend to the story of André Pagnol's adultery in *Le Temps des secrets*) or because he was increasingly absorbed by other projects — he now began to take an interest in the possibilities of television — that he never completed the *Souvenirs*. But he had yet to give his memories a final shape by the time of his death in 1974. Fallois, his friend and publisher, assembled what he had written and *Le Temps des amours* was duly published posthumously in 1977. The story of Marcel's happy school-days is continued until he is fourteen. He makes friends, recalls his teachers with gentle irony, still plays roles and is no less protective towards Augustine. But he is older now and more independent — Joseph's success in the *pétanque* tournament at La Treille in 1907, though a triumph, cannot be a new 'gloire' — and his passion for words prompts clear literary ambitions. Less rich in imagery and comic invention, *Le Temps des amours* abandons Marcel at the point when he begins to be aware of who he is.

After the success of *La Gloire de mon père*, Clément Pastorelly published little else but Pagnol's works, in handsomely bound copies which regularly sold between 75,000 and 100,000 copies a year. But Pagnol was also available in paperback, and just under a million Pagnol titles were sold annually. In 1986, the first three volumes of the *Souvenirs d'enfance* headed the list, followed by *Topaze*, *Marius*, *Le Temps des amours* and *L'Eau des collines*. Since the success in 1986 of Claude Berri's highly acclaimed films of *Jean de Florette* and *Manon des sources*, Pagnol's only novel has moved several points up the list but failed to dislodge the *Souvenirs* from their number one place.

Pagnol still outsells the ever-popular Zola and few best-selling authors have known such longevity. His plays are revived on the Paris stage and when his films are screened on television, audience ratings are high. But his autobiography clearly occupies a special niche in French affections. But is 'autobiography' the right word? It has been described as a literary 'hybrid' and doubts about the 'truth' and 'accuracy' of Pagnol's memories have often been expressed. Readers and critics frequently conclude that the work is 'une autobiographie romancée' — and none the worse for that, of course. But the question is an interesting one, for it affects the way we read what Pagnol has to say. In what proportions is it 'autobiography' and to what extent is it fiction? How much human truth is contained in these two volumes which are clearly designed to entertain? Before we can answer such questions, we must consider the matter of form.

Why does anyone write autobiography? Autobiographers write out of curiosity or set out to justify themselves, take revenge on others or, more philosophically, to understand their successive selves and illuminate the collective experience of the human condition. On the other hand, politicians recount their part in historical events, actors polish their public image with carefully measured glimpses of their private lives, writers and artists tell of their struggles and aspirations... There are as many reasons for writing autobiography as there are autobiographers.

Of course, a life may be told whole or in part and recollections of childhood are numerous. Richard Coe used the term 'a Childhood' to describe such 'early lives' and identified over 600 examples written in many different kinds of ink. *Poil de carotte* (1894) is a bitter exorcism of Jules Renard's unhappy home life. Maxim Gorky's harrowing memories of his *Childhood* (1913) amount to an indictment of the ethos of Tsarist Russia. In quite a different mood, Dylan Thomas's *Portrait of the Artist as a Young Dog* (1940) positively revels in those first bright discoveries of the world outside his head. Laurie Lee's *Cider with Rosie* (1959) re-creates if not all the facts, then at least the feel of his past. A 'Childhood' covers everything from the laying of ghosts to the joyous celebration of the fun of it all, via sober re-enactments of child psychology (the world 're-created through the eyes of a child'), earnest accounts of apprenticeships in lifeskills and attempts to recapture a unique experience or a world that has passed away. The genre is not easily defined.

Of course, a distinction must be made between autobiography proper and writing that is 'autobiographical'. If 'Madame Bovary, c'est moi', as Flaubert said, shall we conclude that her story is also his? The most famous 'childhood' in French literature, Alain-

Fournier's *Le Grand Meaulnes* (1913), is cast as a novel. *David Copperfield* borrows heavily on Dickens's own childhood experiences, yet is classed as a novel because the autobiographical element is not indulged for its own sake but is used for another purpose: as background to the story of the fictional David.

On the other hand, recollections of public figures which tell of public events rather than private concerns are to be classed as 'Memoirs' rather than autobiography which, properly speaking, gives pride of place to the intimate biography of the author and is concerned with establishing a personal identity. As Georges May (*3*, p.123) expresses it, 'Memoirs' contain the 'récit de ce qu'on a vu ou entendu, de ce qu'on a fait ou dit' whereas autobiography is the 'récit de ce qu'on a été'.

The distinction is rarely clear-cut, however, for self-portraitists may be moved simultaneously by conflicting motives — to tell an exemplary tale, to set the record straight, to find meaning in the past or simply to relive it. In formal terms, an autobiography is generally a first-person narrative which unfolds chronologically, though some writers use an alias and free-wheel through time. The objective is honesty, though truth is endangered not only by memory, which is notoriously defective, but by conscious or unconscious distortions aimed at hiding part of the self or at protecting the innocent; by irony and playfulness which are generally signs of a degree of insincerity; and, not least, by the temptations of art which shapes the basic material and uses techniques drawn from other kinds of writing, such as the novel.

Richard Coe takes the discussion closer to the case of Pagnol in his study of the 'Childhood' which, without being strictly speaking a literary genre, has identifiable characteristics. It:

i) assumes the uniqueness of the experience of childhood which is conveyed through the sense of wonder, the discovery of the world and the power of the child's imagination;

ii) concedes that first memories, though sharpest of all, may mislead (because they are disjointed, or distorted by childish misunderstandings) and leave gaps many authors readily fill with inventions which, though they may not be authentic, are consistent with their feelings about their past;

iii) attempts to convey the magic of existence from the child's point of view by demonstrating how he/she makes sense of life by imposing patterns upon it, by showing a fascination for words (to name an object is to possess it) or by living a make-believe life drawn from story-books (to transform an experience is to master it);

iv) recognises the existence of archetypal figures. Fathers are generally cruel/domineering or ineffectual/dead, and mothers sometimes hateful but more often futile, weak, but much loved. There may be a marginal person — a grandmother, aunt or teacher — who proves to be a major influence for good, or a bully or tyrant who symbolises evil;

v) gives due place to archetypal experiences: the child's sense of timelessness, its cruelty (to animals, for example), its rebelliousness, the first inklings of sex or injustice, the problem of lying, the sense of theatre (which includes superstitions and tribal rituals), and the idea of death as something foreign which happens to other people;

vi) defines the child's world as geographically small but shows that everything in it is big, boundless even: the death of a pet, the first pair of football boots, a fleeting friendship or a trifling event make that world authentic, while trivial personal memories such as the names of sweets or famous 'firsts' (the first goal, lie, kiss) conjure up a world that is not merely authentic, or mysterious, but wider, freer and better than the world of adulthood.

'Childhoods' are qualitatively different from other kinds of autobiography because our early experiences have a special, but not always pleasant, meaning for each one of us: few of us have been famous generals or actresses, but we have all been children and remember the pains and joys of the experience. In anthropological terms, childhood is a necessary flexing of muscles which prepares the fledgling to face the world alone. Sociologists see it as part of the socialising process which turns anarchical children into conforming adults. For linguisticians, the acquisition of language means mastering the world, for when we can give things a name we make them ours. Freudians view our early years as the seed-bed of our later personality. But all agree on the 'otherness' of children and make the 'play' element — the make-believe, the odd rules of children's games — the quality which makes childhood especially fascinating. And reading about other people's childhoods puts us in touch with our own forgotten, pre-social selves.

'Early lives' are qualitatively different from even the most sympathetic stories written by adults about children. Roald Dahl's *Danny, Champion of the World* (1975), like Pagnol's *Souvenirs d'enfance*, deals with an eight-year-old boy and his relationship with his father; the two live 'in the country' and draw closer during a hunt for game birds. Beside Marcel's, Danny's world seems limited and his story, because it *is* a story, has a neat, manufactured feel to it. Pagnol's scope for invention was limited by the facts of his life which we accept as true in a way that Danny's are not: Marcel's experiences belong to a different order of lived, rather than imagined reality.

The difference between the 'Childhood' and the 'novel of childhood' is far from clear. Some of the most effective 'childhoods' have been written as fiction, from Dickens and Mark Twain to Sue Townsend, from Jules Vallès to Annie Leclerc. Like the 'Childhood' proper, they support the view, which has been accepted only since the eighteenth century, that our formative years are a special time. English and American cultures have been especially strong in books written about and for children. In comparison, the French have never dwelt on their childhood days with quite the same delighted enthusiasm and it will come as no surprise therefore that in 1977 the most popular author with French under-thirteens, with 35 million copies sold in twenty years, was Enid Blyton.

The vogue for the 'Childhood' has expanded enormously since 1945 and Pagnol's *Souvenirs d'enfance* clearly fall into a general cultural pattern. Yet in many ways, they broke new ground. Reviewing *La Gloire de mon père*, Dominique Fernandez wrote:

> Si je pense à Stevenson, à Mark Twain, à Gorki, je
> m'aperçois que la littérature française est totalement

> incapable de décrire cet émerveillement trépidant et
> amusé qui est le propre d'un jeune garçon découvrant le
> monde. Voilà cette lacune comblée. (*11*, p.328)

It is significant that of the three authors mentioned here, two are
novelists. Indeed, Marcel often seems much closer to Tom Sawyer
and the Jim Hawkins of *Treasure Island* than to French models like
Jules Vallès's Jacques Vingtras, Daudet's Daniel Eyssette or Jules
Renard's Poil de carotte. Of course all in their own ways set out to
tell the truth. But what kind of truth? Should we prefer the writer's
imaginative licence to the duller objective narration of verifiable
facts? Pagnol's 'Childhood' is very different from the account of his
early years given by his biographer Raymond Castans, for Pagnol
does not aim to provide the same kind of 'documentary' survey. On
the contrary, the way he tells his story betrays his playwright's ear
for dialogue and his film-maker's eye for the dramatic situation.
When, in a television interview in 1962, Pagnol was asked by Jean
Demayet to what extent his 'Childhood' was a novel, he replied:

> Ça doit l'être un peu, mais je ne m'en suis pas aperçu en
> l'écrivant. J'ai eu l'impression de raconter les choses
> comme elles se sont passées. Et, pourtant, elles ne se
> sont sûrement pas passées comme ça, puisque vous
> pouvez lire en deux heures le récit de deux ans. Il a fallu
> inconsciemment resserrer, condenser. En tout cas, ce qui
> est rigoureusement exact, ce sont les détails, mais peut-
> être que l'ensemble ne l'est pas tout à fait. (*11*, p.330)

But if the parts are true, how can the whole be false? How shall we
know if Pagnol is re-creating his past as honestly as he can, or
betraying it with his talent to amuse?

2. Pagnol as Chronicler

Much of Pagnol's work (and a good part of his charm) is rooted in nostalgia. The schoolboy who published his first poems in the local newspaper *Massilia* in 1909 revealed a precocious awareness of the classical past. The serial story, *Les Mémoires de Jacques Panier* which he wrote for *Fortunio*, a kind of undergraduate magazine run by Pagnol and like-minded school friends, looked back to the camaraderie of his years at the Lycée Thiers at Marseilles. 'Ces mémoires sont de véritables mémoires: toutes les pages en furent dictées le soir, au coin du feu, tandis que, les yeux clos, je regardais passer mes souvenirs' (*Pirouettes* (1932), p.11). They were not, needless to say, 'true memoirs', but the retrospective habit was already firmly established.

Of course, the first writings of many authors draw heavily on their own past, but memory always played a central role in Pagnol's creative processes. His prefaces to *Catulle* and *Pirouettes* evoke with affection 'le jeune homme pauvre que je fus', just as the 'mémorialiste' of the *Souvenirs d'enfance* pays tribute to 'l'enfant que je ne suis plus. C'est un petit personnage que j'ai connu, et qui s'est fondu dans l'air du temps à la manière des oiseaux qui disparaissent sans laisser de squelette' (*Gloire*, p.7). But even the Pagnol who satirised contemporary manners in the 1920s was keenly aware of what lay over his shoulder. The plots of *Les Marchands de gloire* and *Jazz* were based on anecdotes told to him by his father and his father's friends, and Joseph is present at several different levels in *Topaze*. Indeed, all of Pagnol's 'intellectuals' from Topaze to Jean de Florette owe a considerable debt to Pagnol senior. And in a wider sense, the films set in Marseilles and the hills of Lower Provence all hark back to a kind of golden age when people were less materialistic and more kindly and the world was a simpler place — the world of his youth.

Backward-looking by temperament, Pagnol never lost touch with his roots and spent as much of his time in the Midi as possible. Yet it was not until relatively late in life that he took openly to autobiography, and even then did so in a most limited way: the four volumes of the *Souvenirs d'enfance* cover only the first fourteen years of his life. Yet in a sense, he had already dealt with his adolescence in the *Fortunio* stories, for their hero, the ebullient and articulate Jacques Panier, is a version of Pagnol himself. They preserve the mood and flavour of his early manhood, though they reveal nothing specific about his university studies, his precocious marriage in 1916, his experience of teaching, the impact of the Great War, his brother's illness or his subsequent relationship with his father. But of course Jacques Panier is not Pagnol: he is the hero of a selectively autobiographical novel.

More factual, but no more revealing of Pagnol's personality, were the prefaces, written in 1963 for his *Œuvres complètes*, which continued the story of his life. Republished posthumously in one volume in 1981, they remain silent on his private affairs and, though entitled *Confidences*, confide very little of his inner self which, to the end, he kept carefully hidden. Jacques Panier had written 'mémoires', not autobiography, and Pagnol the 'préfacier' followed suit. It is true that when friends like Raimu died, he wrote soberly of his sense of loss. But he rarely spoke directly of his personal feelings, preferring to shelter behind the stories of his plays and films, revealing nothing of the events which touched the rawest nerves, such as the tragic death of his daughter at the age of two in 1954. *Confidences* is a volume of literary memoirs and, though a fascinating and necessary complement to his imaginative work, does not pretend to be a self-portrait.

Pagnol's reticence was not so much an effect of modesty as a wish to preserve his privacy. Rarely do prominent figures protect their private lives quite so carefully, for most accept that they are to some extent public property. Even during the thirties, when his star status made him fair game for journalists seeking to satisfy the curiosity of readers eager for back-stage glimpses of their idols, he gave little away — save to confide that when he was young he wanted to be a boxer. Thirty years later, he was still making it clear to journalists (see above, p.14) that he disliked 'confidences': 'il ne faut pas trop parler de sa vie privée'. There is no reason therefore why we should expect the *Souvenirs d'enfance* to be a frank and intimate confession. But what does Pagnol tell us of the facts?

He tells us that his paternal grandfather, André Pagnol, a stonemason by trade, was born at Valréas (in either 1819 or 1830 according to *Le Temps des secrets*, pp.26, 29, 38), married in 1845 and fathered six children, four of whom became *instituteurs*, though Pagnol mentions only Marie, headmistress of a primary school at La Ciotat, Joséphine, who became head of a girls' *école supérieure* in Marseilles and was prominent in local causes (*Secrets*, pp.25-26), and Joseph. *Le Temps des amours* further reveals that André spent a year in Paris (1871-72) repairing the Hôtel de Ville after the damage caused by the Paris Commune. With his wife Eugénie, he retired to a farm near Roquevaire and died in 1907.

Pagnol's maternal grandfather, Auguste Lansot, was born in 1845 at Coutances and died in South America in 1869 when he was twenty-four. He had three children: Henri, a mechanic, Rose and Augustine.

In 1889, Joseph Pagnol, after training at the 'école normale' at Aix, became an *instituteur*, or primary school teacher, at Aubagne where he met and married a seamstress, Augustine Lansot. Marcel was delivered by the midwife Mme Négrel at 16 Cours Barthélémy. His brother Paul followed in 1898 by which time the family had moved to the outskirts of Marseilles when Joseph was appointed to the staff of a primary school at Saint-Loup. In October 1900, Joseph moved again, to the Ecole du Chemin des Chartreux where Marcel enrolled as a pupil. To supplement his income, Joseph took on additional work, in particular collaborating with a colleague named Arnaud who prepared classroom maps for the publisher Vidal-Lablache. At about this time, Marcel was taken for walks in the park by his aunt Rose who met and married uncle Jules/Thomas. Two years later, 'la petite soeur' was born, a year before the first summer spent at La Treille which occurred when Marcel was eight (i.e., 1903). Joseph joined forces with Jules to rent La Bastide Neuve and the 'été des bartavelles' unfolds, made even more memorable by the meeting with Lili, until it is time to return to school.

The school year culminates in Marcel's success in the scholarship examination in what is not 1904 but 1905, for Marcel is now ten, though the chronology requires him to be nine. The story of the 'quatre châteaux' occurs in July and volume two ends just before Marcel starts school at the Lycée. A brief coda reveals that five years later (1909 or 1910, therefore) Augustine died. She was followed by Lili in 1917 and by Paul 'à trente ans' (i.e., 1928). 'Ten years' later (i.e., 1938), Pagnol set up his own film company and bought the Château which had filled his mother with fear.

Pagnol's own account of his early years is broadly accurate, but it omits or minimises many facts which a biographer would wish to record. Since part of the pleasure of reading biography and autobiography is a measure of healthy voyeurism, readers may be curious to be put more fully into the picture in order to see what Pagnol left out of his recollections of his early life. The following chronology supplements the facts which Pagnol gives:

1864 Birth of Thomas Jaubert ('oncle Jules') who died in 1941.
      Birth of Marie Pagnol ('tante Marie').
1867 Birth of Adolphe Pagnol who in 1895 was teaching with
      Joseph at the Ecole Lakanal in Aubagne, where he still worked
      in 1904.
1868 Birth of Joséphine, the formidable 'Fifi' of *Le Temps des
      secrets*, and headmistress of a primary school in Marseilles. As
      Mme Colombelle, she became one of the most militant
      feminists in the Midi.
1869 25 October: birth of Joseph André Pagnol at Vaison-la-
      Romaine.
1873 Birth of Augustine Pauline Henriette Lansot.
1877(?) Death of Auguste Lansot.
1886 October - January 1889: Joseph Pagnol, aged 17, enters the
      Ecole normale des Bouches-du-Rhône at Aix-en-Provence.

After graduating, he did three months' teaching practice in a school at La Cabucelle, a tough district of Marseilles. On 1 January 1889, his excellent examination results earned a good first appointment at the Ecole Lakanal, the elementary school at Aubagne. He lived in a room on the premises.

1893 Marriage of Joseph Pagnol and Augustine Lansot, a seamstress, at her aunt Virginie Lansot's property at Sabatery near Marseilles. Though Augustine was a practising Catholic, Joseph insisted on a civil wedding. They began their married life in a third-floor flat at 16, Cours Barthélémy at Aubagne.

1894 28 April: birth of Maurice Pagnol, who died aged four months on 18 August.

1895 28 February: birth of Marcel-Paul Pagnol, at 5 p.m. The midwife Mme Négrel was the wife of a hat-maker: she was paid 13 francs and remembered the birth clearly when Pagnol met her by accident in 1937. Joseph was 26 and Augustine 22. The witnesses were Joseph's brother Adolphe and Auguste Arnaud, also *instituteurs* at the Ecole Lakanal. According to the newspapers, it was a very cold and snowy day. Only a few hours earlier, the Lumière brothers filmed the famous sequence of a train entering the station at La Ciotat: Pagnol later remarked that he was as old as cinema.

1896 12 April: Marcel-Paul Pagnol was baptised, without Joseph's knowledge, at the Church of Saint Charles where his mother worshipped. His godparents were Pauline Lansot, his grandmother, and Henri Lansot, his uncle.

1897 October: Joseph appointed to the school at Saint-Loup. Saint-Loup, half-way between Aubagne and Marseilles, was still in the country and Joseph grew his own vegetables and Augustine kept chickens. A school at Saint-Loup, the 'lycée Marcel Pagnol', was inaugurated on 7 October 1962.

1898 28 April: birth of Paul Pagnol who died in 1932, aged 34. He suffered from 'le haut-mal', a form of epilepsy. After attending agricultural college, he subsequently withdrew to La Treille and became 'le dernier chévrier de Virgile'. Pagnol dedicated his translation of Virgil's *Bucoliques* (1957) to Paul who probably taught him more about the flora and fauna of the hills than anyone else.

1900   1 June: Joseph appointed to the staff of the Ecole du Chemin des Chartreux, the largest primary school in Marseilles: it had a staff of eleven.

October: Joseph takes up his new post and Marcel starts school.

At first, they lived in a flat on the premises before moving to the rue du Jardin des Plantes. To supplement his income, Joseph gave private lessons, kept accounts for local tradesmen and collaborated with Auguste Arnaud (who had also transferred to the Ecole du Chemin des Chartreux) in the preparation of classroom maps.

1902   2 February: birth of Germaine Pagnol, 'la petite soeur'. Shortly afterwards, the Pagnols move to 33, rue de Tivoli.

1903   Birth of Pierre Jaubert, son of Rose and 'Jules', who trained as a notary. After the Second World War, he became a farmer in the Roussillon.

July: The Pagnols and the Jauberts take a villa near La Treille for several seasons. Eventually, they stopped using La Bastide Neuve and rented another villa nearby called Ravel at the foot of the Barres Saint-Esprit. Marcel meets Lili, whose real name was David Magnan.

1905   July: Pagnol sits the 'scholarship' examination.

1905   October: Pagnol starts school at the Lycée Thiers as a *demi-pensionnaire* or day-boarder.

Opening of the tramway link between Marseilles and Aubagne.

1906   The Pagnols move to 51, rue Terrusse, then to No. 52 which was just round the corner. In all, the restless Joseph lived at seventeen different addresses before finally settling at 8, cours Julien where he remained for twenty years.

His anticlericalism notwithstanding, Joseph pays a neighbour at 33, rue de Tivoli, the abbé Gouin, former curé of Les Accates, to give Marcel extra Latin lessons.

Around this time, Joseph, to supplement his income, teaches at

the Ecole de Commerce de Marseille. He seems to have
remained at the Ecole des Chartreux until 1912 when he left
the state sector and taught in a number of private schools.
He returned to elementary schools in 1918, at the time of the
severe post-war teacher-shortage, and ended his career as head
of the school in the rue Sainte-Pauline in Marseilles.

1907 Extension of a branch line of the tramway from La Barrasse
to Les Camoins.
Death of André Pagnol.

1909 25 July: birth of René Pagnol.

1910 15 June: Augustine dies of pulmonary congestion, aged 37.
She was buried in the cemetery of Saint-Pierre at Marseilles in
the Jaubert family vault.

1911 Joseph hires a housekeeper who has a friend called Madeleine
Jullien, also a widow, who helps her on occasions.

1912 30 July: Joseph marries Madeleine Jullien and modifies his
anticlericalism. The marriage took place in church and
Joseph became an English teacher in a private Catholic school,
the Pension Chaix.

1916 After passing the two stages of the 'baccalauréat' (1912,
'mention passable' and 1913 'mention assez bien'), Pagnol
graduates with a degree in English from Montpellier
University. The same year, he marries Simone-Thérèse-
Félicité Collin against the wishes of his father. The marriage
was dissolved in 1941.

1918 23 July: death of Lili (David Magnan) at Vrigny (Marne) in
the trenches of World War One. His brother Baptistin Magnan
died shortly afterwards of a fever contracted during military
service in the Far East.

1932 Death of Paul in a Belgian clinic.

1933 Pagnol sets up his own company, Les Films Marcel Pagnol,
and becomes the most successful independent film-maker of
the 1930s.

1941 21 July: Pagnol buys La Buzine and its 37 hectares of grounds
with a view to converting the property into cinema studios.
One of a number of châteaux in the valley of the Huveaune, it

was built just before the war of 1870 by a Marseilles entre-
preneur named Hilaire Courtil. A former owner, Henri de
Buzin, had given it its name. During the war, the château was
occupied by the Germans. After the Liberation it was requisi-
tioned by the French Army and was subsequently occupied by
Spanish refugee families who remained in residence for six-
teen years. During this time, the house and grounds were
neglected and badly damaged and it cost more than the com-
pensation offered by the government to effect urgent repairs.
In 1972, Pagnol returned for the last time to La Buzine during
the filming of a series of interviews for French television. A
year before his death, he sold the property to a developer,
though Mme Germaine Gombert continued to live there until
1975. It was finally demolished in the early 1980s.
August: death of Thomas Jaubert, who was buried at Saint-
Pierre in Marseilles.

1951   8 November: death of Joseph Pagnol at the Château de Buzine.
He was interred at La Treille with his second wife. Augustine's
remains had been transferred from Saint-Pierre to La Treille
and Estelle Pagnol (1952-54), Pagnol's daughter, was buried
with her as was, in 1974, Pagnol himself.

A comparison of this historical record with the first two volumes of
Pagnol's autobiography is revealing. The fact that a few of his dates
are wrong (Lili was killed in action in 1918 not 1917) or approxi-
mate (Paul died in 1932 not 1928 and Les Films Marcel Pagnol was
established in 1933 not 1938 as the text suggests) indicates that
Pagnol was not unduly concerned with accuracy. More significantly,
the chronology is confused: Marcel's ninth year is missing
altogether, for the first summer at La Treille is in fact the summers
of 1903 and 1904 rolled into one. And when Pagnol's 'facts' can be
checked, they sometimes prove to be wrong: primary school teachers
were not well paid but earned more than the 54 francs Pagnol puts in
Joseph's wage-packet, while the story of the abbé Barthélémy loses
its neatness when we know that he occupied not seat number 25 in
the French Academy but number 19.

Also interesting are the omissions. There is no obvious reason why Pagnol should have deliberately covered up his secret baptism which Augustine hid from the anti-clerical Joseph — indeed, it has the makings of an archetypal Pagnol story — nor need we be surprised by the absence of grandparents and other members of the family, like Adolphe Pagnol who was still teaching at Aubagne in 1904, because they clearly did not loom large in Marcel's life. Marie Pagnol and Henri Lansot have walk-on parts and Joséphine appears briefly in *Le Temps des secrets* where old André Pagnol and his wife are also shown squabbling. But their absence confirms what seems to have been the case: Marcel grew up in a family atmosphere that was more nuclear than extended.

Of greater significance, however, is Pagnol's failure to mention the death of the Pagnols' first-born,. Maurice, or the cruel form of epilepsy from which Paul suffered, for omissions such as these reveal Pagnol's reluctance to speak openly of the darker side of his memories. The sight he gives of Augustine, though glowingly idealised, is nevertheless monochrome. She has the passivity and vulnerability which characterise most of the female leads of his plays and films who are ultimately the object of male protectiveness: even the most liberated and active of them, Manon des sources, is finally tamed by love and reduced to a state of stereotyped domestication. Admirers of Pagnol's later work might well suspect therefore that Augustine is less a picture of the author's mother than yet another character invented for literary purposes.

In the same way, there is scarcely a hint of the later differences which made Pagnol's relationship with his father more fraught than his genial narrative implies. It is surely significant that Joseph, who died in 1951 only five years before Pagnol composed his *Souvenirs*, is not commemorated in the coda to *Le Château de ma mère* along with Lili, Paul and Augustine whose loss Pagnol sincerely grieved. Twice he suggests that Joseph had a roving eye and on both occasions it is caught by bakers' wives: but the suggestion is not allowed to ruffle Joseph's image as model husband and father and is quickly dismissed as an 'idée déplaisante... que je n'ai jamais acceptée' (*Gloire*, p.23; cf. *Amours*, p.102) — though it may well have contributed something to the way Pagnol later conceived his film *La Femme du boulanger* (1938). As an adolescent, Pagnol reacted against Joseph's second marriage and himself married against his father's wishes. The Oedipal antagonism of son and father surely existed, for it later surfaces in the criticism of Joseph's moralistic naïvety implicit in *Topaze* and more clearly still in the tensions which arise between Marius and César in the Marseilles trilogy. Pagnol himself recognised in Marius a reflection of 'cette rupture qui se produit entre le fils qui est devenu un homme et le père qui continue à le considérer comme un enfant' (*9*, pp.34-35). Behind the open-hearted idealists of all Pagnol's fictions lies the stubborn, obsessive, abrasive innocence of Joseph against which Pagnol measured his own worldly success. The evidence suggests that his father was not always the jovial, solid pillar of permanence of Pagnol's written recollections.

Pagnol's memories of childhood are clearly neither complete nor exact but they also exude a distinct whiff of art. He once revealed that his old friend Marius Brouquier, the stonemason at La Treille who built the village used for shooting the film *Regain* (1937), occasionally wrote him letters in fractured French: to spare his feelings, Pagnol replied in kind (*9*, pp.231-32). It is impossible to say whether Pagnol's letters to his friend imitated Marcel's reply to Lili, or whether he used the ploy retrospectively for effect, just as he does several times in his novel *L'Eau des collines*. What makes us suspect that the second is quite likely to be the case is that Pagnol can occasionally be caught 'en flagrant délit de fausse mémoire'. Thus members of La Société des Amis de Marcel Pagnol at La Treille in the 1950s believed that Bouzigue was not described from memory but bore a striking resemblance to Victor Sorrentino, the Society's president (*7*, p.254).

But even more difficult than the lure of literary licence was the unreliability of memory. In *Le Temps des amours* (pp.129-30), he tells how, at the age of thirteen, he made a new friend, Yves. To impress him, he told him the story of Joseph's 'coup du roi': 'Cette épopée — à mon insu — s'était grandement enrichie, pour avoir été trente fois mise sur le métier: le poids et les dimensions des perdrix royales avaient doublé, mon père les avait abattues à plus de cent mètres, et, en les recevant sur la tête, je m'étais évanoui, dans une mare de sang.' How much more difficult it must have been, then, at the age of sixty, however clearly his impressions were etched in his mind, to recall the simple truth, and how great the temptation for a supreme raconteur to embroider and improve what he did remember.

Of course, as a 'mémorialiste', Pagnol does not claim to tell the whole truth: Marcel's story 'n'est qu'un témoignage sur une époque disparue, et une petite chanson de piété filiale' (*Gloire*, p.10). If all tension and bitterness are removed from his childhood and his parents are washed whiter than white, it is because Pagnol chose deliberately to present his past uncensoriously, as many others have done, like Edward Blishen who described his strategy in an image Pagnol would have approved of: 'I have been along the overgrown hedges of reality, trimming them to let the light in, and have given its ditches a rather easier flow than they actually had' (*A Cack-handed War*, 1972). Pagnol's 'filial piety' gives a quite legitimate cast to his private world. But to what extent are his *Souvenirs* a 'témoignage sur une époque disparue'?

La Gloire de mon père begins in firm documentary vein. After a brief guided tour of family history, Pagnol explains why old André considered education to be the Sovereign Good and what it meant to young men and women like Joseph and Marie (*Gloire*, pp.14-20). Pagnol's account of the *instituteur* ethic, though correct in outline, is heavily ironic. Jules Ferry's education acts (1881-83) had made primary education free, compulsory and secular. Their purpose was clear: the new Third Republic, shakily inaugurated after the Commune of 1871, sought to remove education from the hands of the Church and turn it into a means of realising one of the central aims of the French Revolution, 'la carrière ouverte aux talents'. By 1890, there were 143,000 primary school teachers and over 5 million pupils in their classes. As a piece of social engineering, it was remarkably successful, for it released the abilities of a generation of clever children of poor parents who hitherto had been denied the means of self-improvement.

After passing the *certificat d'études primaires* at 12 and the *brevet élémentaire* at 15, Joseph, like his brother and sisters, stayed on at school for an extra year to prepare for entry to the *école normale* where they trained as *instituteurs* or primary school teachers. 'Primary' education, a level of education and not an age division, was designed to provide a basic training in a wide range of mainly practical subjects. 'Secondary' education, available in the *lycée*, offered more academic subjects, like science and Latin, and was the road to university and the liberal professions. Part of the tension between Joseph and Jules derives precisely from the fact that while Jules had received a secondary education, Joseph had not: hence both his determination to ensure that his son should be given an opportunity which he had been denied and the jubilation which greets Marcel's success in the 'scholarship' examination which enables him to move from the *primaire* to the *secondaire* which offered a whole new world of opportunities. In roughly equivalent terms, Pagnol was a 'grammar-school' success, and he remained grateful to the Third Republic which had given him the chance which he had gladly taken.

The products of the 'normal colleges' saw themselves not simply as teachers but as heralds of a new social order based on justice and the rights of man. They were normally fierce champions of Republican values and stood firm against privilege, royalism and the Church which they regarded as forces of reaction and obscurantism. Pay and conditions of service were poor and Pagnol's picture of their painful progress from the 'hameaux perdus' to 'la plaine' and even to the 'chef-lieu', is quite accurate. They earned between 75 and 125 francs a month, less than postmen and some manual workers who were paid 6 francs a day. They taught classes of up to sixty, went in awe of headmasters and inspectors and faced a barrage of criticism from the Church and the middle-classes who regarded them as a subversive influence — which many were proud to be. For, in addition to teaching the three Rs, they promoted the 'socialist' values of parliamentary democracy and universal suffrage, denounced war, stated their faith in progress and science, supported campaigns to improve basic hygiene and combat alcoholism, and took the view that only an educated population could be saved from the evils of poverty and ignorance. Heirs of the French Revolution and of the scientific positivism of the nineteenth century, they were, in Péguy's phrase, 'les hussards noirs de la République' and felt part of a crusade to improve the moral and material lives of the children in their care. Having themselves only recently emerged from poverty, at considerable financial sacrifice to their families, they knew that education was the key to the future.

Pagnol writes of them with affectionate irony. He caricatures their naïve faith in their 'mission', their one-sided view of *curés*, popes and monarchs, and their concept of the French Revolution as 'une explosion de bonté'. He gently mocks their preoccupation with alcoholism by describing in wickedly lurid terms the horrific pictures of diseased livers hanging on their classroom walls and he neatly captures their prejudices in a bottle: a digestive liqueur, made by monks and sold 'avec privilège du Roy', represented, 'dans une trinité atroce, l'Eglise, l'Alcool et la Royauté'. But if Pagnol seems to score some cheap points, he redresses the balance by noting that many *curés* regarded the Holy Inquisition, which broke bodies in order to save souls, as 'une sorte de Conseil de Famille', and he shakes his head sorrily over the intolerance shown on both sides by remarking, in the manner of La Rochefoucauld, that reason 'ne sert le plus souvent qu'à justifier nos croyances'. He even shares their suspicion of the establishment by observing that 'tous les manuels d'histoire du monde n'ont jamais été que des livrets de propagande au service des gouvernements' (*Gloire*, p.16). Pagnol seems as opposed to the excesses of the Church, which claimed a moral monopoly, as he was to the *instituteurs*' exclusive educational ideal of 'laïcité' (the principle that education should be managed by and for the State regardless of the claims of religion). The overall impression he gives is far from unsympathetic to the primary school teachers and Pagnol, who was raised in their world, pays a genuine tribute to their personal idealism and disinterestedness: 'Ils avaient une foi totale dans la beauté de leur mission, une confiance radieuse dans l'avenir de la race humaine' (*ib.*, p.19). And Joseph is given the last word: like his colleagues, he worked to build a just future in this world.

Joseph, a first-generation *instituteur*, is in many ways typical of the breed. He is shown to be a pious teetotaller and a relentlessly 'grand pédagogue' (*Gloire*, p.110), somewhat given to delivering 'conférences politico-sociales' (*ib.*, p.79). His anti-clericalism, expressed more in words than in deeds, is fierce. He does not care for the name 'les barres de Saint-Esprit' (*ib.*, p.89) which smacks of superstition, and makes remarks 'avec une certaine joie laïque' about the appropriately named merciless praying mantis (*ib.*, p.106). His political views are distinctly radical. He denounces private property and indeed berates the Republic for permitting it (*ib.*, p.79.). But most of his ideas are expressed in his furious clashes with the *lycée*-educated, right-wing, Catholic Jules who worked as a clerk in the Town Hall. Pagnol uses their differences less to throw light on the divisions which separated conservative France from the newer progressive doctrines than as a running joke. Joseph lectures Jules on the evils of strong drink (*ib.*, p.95), and they argue furiously about inherited wealth, the intrigues of Radicals, Jesuits, Freemasons and 'M. Comble' (i.e., Emile Combes, 1835-1921) who, as France's Prime Minister, broke the power of the Church and prepared its separation from the state in 1905 (*ib.*, pp.114-15). Jules protests at Joseph's 'matérialisme atroce' and his unbeliever's faith in science (*ib.*, p.119) and complains that holidays should be for children not for teachers. Joseph makes unflattering remarks about idle civil servants, denounces the intolerance of religious fanatics and parades his 'libéralisme' (*ib.*, pp.45-46). As a supplementary joke, their wives grow skilled at devising diversionary tactics designed to keep them apart — so skilled that none of their arguments is developed seriously.

In spite of their differences, Joseph and Jules remain the best of friends and Pagnol cannot be accused of using them to project an accurate historical picture of the political climate of his youth. He makes no reference to specific anti-clerical measures which notably involved the reorganisation of education and, most surprising of all, there is no mention of the Dreyfus affair which had split France politically. François Mauriac (1885-1970) distinctly recalled that in his right-wing bourgeois family a chamber-pot was called a 'zola' out of disrespect for the Dreyfusard Emile Zola who had accused the establishment of covering up an injustice. Jules and Joseph, much less politically aware, seem happy enough to squabble enjoyably over ideological generalities.

In any case, by page 20 of *La Gloire de mon père*, Pagnol's documentary mood evaporates never to return. Outside events of national or local significance do not impinge on Marcel's world. Yet Pagnol's claim to provide 'un témoignage sur une époque disparue' is vindicated in smaller and more subtle ways. He creates a sense of period by occasional reference to everyday objects which are now to be seen only in museums. He lingers over the 'prodigious' storm lantern which lights their meals at La Bastide Neuve (*Gloire*, pp.100-01). Jules's gun is a Verney-Carron (*ib.*, p.135). Joseph owns 'une machine à pédales' and Marcel recalls seeing people learning to ride the newly fashionable bicycle in the Parc Borély (*ib.*, pp.24, 34). Gas lighting, so dear to Rose's heart, was a sign of wealth and modernity, and photographs were a great novelty (*ib.*, p.206). Pagnol lets us into Joseph's classroom and we see Augustine dabbing olive-oil on her children as a precaution against winter chills and against the bronchitis which in those primitive days was 'la maladie redoutable entre toutes' (*Château*, p.64). He gives a clear picture too of how people dressed: the family's 'costume des vacances' (*Gloire*, p.74), the children's winter clothes (*Château*, pp.115-16), Marcel's exam outfit ('col rabattu, cravate à ganse', *ib.*, p.171), Jules's coat of many pockets designed for the well-turned-out hunter and François's greasy jersey and battered cap (*Gloire*, p.75). But his interest in forms of transport is especially effective in evoking the feel of the past. It is a motorless world of walking, and distances have a novel meaning: it is nine kilometres from La Barrasse to Les Bellons and even with the Sunday horse-bus the trek back to Marseilles takes four hours. Hence Pagnol's fascination with handcarts, mules, bogies, horse-drawn removal waggons and the marvellously clanking tram, driven by the 'wattman', which was the latest thing in Progress — until Marcel sees the Gare de l'Est (*Château*, p.117). If the shop of the 'brocanteur' is full of antique oddments, so is Pagnol's memory.

Marcel lives in a world of his own but moves easily between the urban and the rural. Pagnol takes pleasure in reconstructing not only the natural world but in explaining the customs and attitudes of country people. Mond des Parpaillouns wears peculiar clothes, François is not on speaking terms with his brother and no one is handy with a pen. La Bastide Neuve is 200 metres from the village of Les Bellons and we occasionally encounter other villagers: François and his sons Baptistin and Lili, Mme Toffi, M. Vincent the archivist, the postman, the grocer, the curé, plus a crowd of gossiping 'commères' and squabbling *pétanque* players. In the hills, peasants do not interfere with traps set by others and a similar code prevents them hunting on the first day of the season because they despise official permits (*Gloire*, p.182): they regard themselves as hunters and archly define 'poacher' as any outsider (*Château*, p.19). Yet they are not beyond the reach of the law, and they are adept at manipulating rules and regulations, as Bouzigue's victory over the brutal caretaker shows. Yet they so fear the law that an official report of a misdemeanour can lead to murder (*ib*, p.195), the only suggestion here that there is a darker side to their natures. Of course, Marcel is too young to judge such things but even so, just as Jules and Thomas are prevented from coming to blows about politics, so Marcel's memories are protected by strong shock-absorbers from the cruelty and wickedness of people. As he recalls it, 'C'était une époque bénie, où les gens se rendaient service: il n'y avait qu'à demander' (*Gloire*, p.24).

As a chronicle of time past, the *Souvenirs d'enfance* evoke a lost world vividly. Yet as a documentary record it tells us less about the shared experience of a historical period than, say, *Cider with Rosie* or *Poil de carotte*. External reality is much less important than what Marcel (and Pagnol) makes of it, and his autobiography is not the kind of 'témoignage sur une époque disparue' which a social historian would find very useful. On the personal level, Pagnol's playful tone and the omission of painful memories indicate that the process of selection and condensation required part of the hedge to remain standing as a protective screen to hide his deepest feelings. But here, Pagnol gives us fair warning: his autobiography is 'une petite chanson de piété filiale'. This does not mean, however, that what he does say is untrue or that the *Souvenirs d'enfance* amount to an amiable, harmless and 'pious' picture without warts. It is rather that Pagnol, like a guide who points out only the best features of a stately home to those who visit it, lights upon certain kinds of memories. What he once said of Peluque, the larger-than-life, picaresque hero of *Pirouettes*, equally applies to Pagnol the 'mémorialiste':

> ...jamais Peluque n'a menti brutalement. Certes il est souvent difficile, au milieu de ses hyperboles, de discerner la vérité. Elle se déforme étrangement pour qui la voit à travers ce tempérament tumultueux. Mais quant à mentir, c'est-à-dire à créer ou à supprimer un fait dans le passé, Peluque ne l'a jamais fait. (*Pirouettes*, p.46)

Pagnol's truth also hides beneath the 'hyperboles', and he never pretended otherwise. In the Preface to *La Gloire de mon père*, he does not claim to re-create the France of 'M. Comble' but sets out modestly to reflect a private world he once knew intimately: Marcel 'n'est pas le sujet de ce livre, mais le témoin de très petits événements'. Yet Marcel is the glass through which he looks and what we see is refracted through Marcel's personality which is not fixed but changing.

3. Pagnol as Autobiographer

Unlike Epic or Tragedy, autobiography is not a literary genre having a fixed form governed by laws of composition. Writing about the self takes too many shapes for it to be made subject to formal rules. Even so, the autobiographical landscape is marked by features which recur so regularly that they may be said to form permanent landmarks. Self-portraits generally follow chronology and include matters common to the human experience such as the 'shaping influence' (from personal relationships to the impact of public events such as a war) or the 'turning point' (betrayals, successes, failures). In the same way, the 'Childhood', in varying degrees, forms a chronological narrative and includes 'classic' elements of growing awareness and personal development: 'Je suis né, Mon père et ma mère, La maison, Le reste de la famille, Le premier souvenir, Le langage, Le monde extérieur, Les animaux, La mort, Les livres, La vocation, L'école, Le sexe, La fin de l'enfance' (5, p.1033). To this catalogue may be added 'my superstitions, my friends and my lies'.

Pagnol's *Souvenirs d'enfance* touch on all of these subjects — although there are no human deaths until after his childhood days are long over. In the first two volumes in particular he captures what could be preserved of the long-dead Marcel and follows him as he gradually acquires a personality. The 'petits événements' of which he is a witness are recounted not simply to amuse but to chart Marcel's progress as he defines himself against his surroundings.

i) Marcel and Time

The first 'documentary' section of *La Gloire de mon père* sets the tone of semi-detached irony which will dominate Pagnol's reminiscences. But it also has the function of fixing Marcel's existence in time. The account of his family is not offered as a contribution to the social history of France but serves to anchor the arbitrary event of his birth in a continuum of hereditary influences (old André's hammer-head symbolises the legacy of practical skills which Pagnol inherited) and moral attitudes (the belief in education and the uprightness of Joseph's training). Although the story of Pagnol's birth is of necessity told at second hand, it creates a sense of beginning which puts a different value on time, for Marcel is now part of the flow of human existence. His first active memories are disjointed — he remembers sitting in Joseph's classroom, his mother's fears that his brain will explode, the abattoir across the road, his pleasure in working Augustine's sewing machine — and Pagnol is able to date such happenings only by reference to external events such as Joseph's move to Saint-Loup in 1897 or Paul's birth in 1898. The start of primary school and Rose's meeting with Jules, when he is five or six, are stronger points of reference because the memory of them is clearer. But Marcel's speculations about how babies are born or his misunderstanding of the ideological 'escarmouches amicales' of Jules and Joseph are designed to show how little sense he still makes of what goes on around him. But until April 1903, when he is eight and on the verge of the first summer at Les Bellons (*Gloire*, p.53), Marcel does not acquire a sense of chronology. Pagnol occasionally notes his age or refers to a month as a way of giving the reader a bearing, but the flow of time is distorted by what he remembers. His childhood is made up of stretches of time when nothing happens at all interspersed with brief moments made long by the intensity of his involvement. Time means nothing to Marcel until his desires give it a meaning. Thus the task of repairing the furniture lasted just three months but occupies 'dans ma mémoire une place considérable' because it was then that he discovered 'l'intelligence de mes mains' (*ib.*, p.69). The end of July becomes significant because it sees the start of the holiday, and 15 August because it marks the opening of the hunting season. But the word 'avenir' still means 'later the same day' (*ib.*, p.76). The 'été des bartavelles' is timeless and Marcel lives in an eternal present. He is detached from his past at Marseilles and the distant future is unreal.

If he ever returns to school, it will be 'vers la fin des temps' (*ib.*, p.116) and Jules's talk of his entry to the *lycée* is incomprehensible because it concerns 'les siècles futurs' (*Château*, p.53).

But his appalled realisation that October and the end of the holidays are upon him marks the end of a phase: he ceases to exist outside time and enters a less glamorous world ruled by the calendar. His immunity vanishes and the demands of reality remove his privileged status. He is forced to watch the school year unfold slowly through the Christmas at La Treille, February, April, May and June (which brings the scholarship exam) until it culminates on 1 August with Joseph's humiliation at the hands of the disagreeable caretaker. Marcel has learnt that his desires are inscribed in time and that he has no choice but to observe its passage which gives his world a ritual pattern and his life a structural framework: the seasons change, new school years start, Paul grows older. Although Pagnol mislays his ninth year, Marcel's growing sense of time turns into a constraint upon his ability to make the world what he chooses it to be: it becomes instead an intimation of mortality. The abrupt coda which closes *Le Château de ma mère* makes the point brutally. Pagnol moves us on rapidly past the death of Augustine, Lili and Paul to 1941 when he bought La Buzine. He discovers that 'trente années avaient dévoré ma vengeance' (*Château*, p.218), but this does not mean that time heals all wounds. On the contrary, time destroys joy and fixes the past in rigid forms which nothing can alter: Augustine's shade will haunt La Buzine in eternal fear. Marcel's awareness of time is a crucial factor in destroying the wonder years.

ii) Marcel and Place

By situating his birth 'aux temps des derniers chevriers', Pagnol identifies his childhood as a foreign land, old in story, where Caesar's legionaries once lit beacons, Roman builders left monuments like the Pont du Gard and the abbé Barthélémy unknowingly blazed a trail for another son of Aubagne. Before Marcel appears on the scene, Pagnol establishes a strong, mysterious sense of place. The urban setting (Aubagne and the suburbs of

Marseilles) in which he grows up is an occasional source of magic
— the old furniture shop is a 'fairy-land' (*Gloire*, p.68) and a ride on
a tram evokes 'un grand mystère' (*ib.*, p.76). But town cicadas sing
'sans la moindre poésie' (*ib.*, p.72) and the magic of place is brilliantly real only in the hills above Les Bellons where Marcel follows
the hunters and which he later explores with Lili. It is a small world,
not much more than four kilometres by ten, but Pagnol charts it in
exact detail. It is dominated by high peaks which look down on flat
plateaux and deep valleys, and their strange names — Garlaban,
Taoumé, Grande Tête Rouge, the valleys of Escouaprés and Passe-
Temps — recur like an incantation. Pagnol mentions over forty such
landmarks which not only reveal his precise topographical knowledge but create a sense of immense size. It is a wild area, large
enough to get lost in, a place of adventure, beauty and danger. In
fact, it is exactly as big as Marcel's imagination, though its magic
does not survive familiarity. As he explores it, it stops being trackless, distances are translated into time (it takes half an hour to walk
from La Bastide Neuve to Le Jas de Baptiste) and daily visits to re-
set snares become routine. The hills grow smaller as Marcel pierces
their secrets. The lesson is clear: we demystify the world even as we
seek to master it. And what is left when all secrets are known?

iii) Marcel and Nature

Pagnol's evocation of nature is very much part of the strong sense of
place. But it is also a prime source of pristine sensations which give
Marcel's world a special quality. There is no crucial moment of
associative memory, no incident as powerful as the tasting of the
madeleine which unlocked Proust's past in vivid colours. But Pagnol
finds regular access to his younger self through his senses, just as
Marcel, when lost with Lili, navigates the befogged landscape by
landmarks known only to his subconscious, 'comme le boeuf qui
rumine trouve dans l'herbe remâchée le goût de graines et de fleurs
qu'il a broutées sans le savoir' (*Château*, p.74). He recalls the smell
of thyme and savory, the brilliant colours of the *limbert*, the cry of
the sparrow-hawk, the taste of almond resin, and the pricks of briar

burrs and the feel of juniper wood which is 'onctueux et lisse' (*ib.*, p.11). Marcel's five acute senses process a world which seems fresh-minted and made especially for him to discover.

His reaction to the plant life he sees for the first time is immediate: 'Je ne savais pas les noms de ces arbres, mais je les aimai aussitôt' (*Gloire*, p.91). But there is no lack of instruction. Joseph weighs in with lectures about donkeys and the *limbert*, Jules with 'doctoral' notes about the *bartavelle* and wild boar, while Lili (who 'savait tout', *Château*, p.28) teaches him the names of plants, animals, birds and all kinds of practical country-lore. With Paul he undertakes those 'observations scientifiques' which involve cruelty to ants and, memorably, to the praying mantis. But it is clear that once again the process of discovery brings ambiguous results: knowledge empties the natural world of much of its magic. As time passes, nature's moods, like the habits of the birds, become predictable and Marcel is able to put a name to everything. As the marvels of nature turn into scientific wonders, so they lose their mystical poetry. It is another instance of the impoverishment which the loss of innocence brings.

iv) Marcel and Books

Of course, Marcel, for whom the world is already a source of infinite variety, comes to La Bastide Neuve expecting perpetual astonishment. He finds it because, like all children, he lives in a world of fantasy: the tram is not a mode of transport but a 'véhicule prodigieux'. But he has been well prepared to meet his change of environment on his own terms, for his responses are very largely shaped by the books he has read.

He has enough imagination to be moved by the stories of Hans Andersen and Alphonse Daudet which he had heard at school but, like most boys of his generation, he preferred the adventures of the detective Nick Carter ('Master of Disguise') and (though in reality they did not appear in print until 1908, five years after Pagnol mistakenly remembers reading about them) the wild escapades of that daring trio 'Les Pieds Nickelés', mainstay of the comic

L'Epatant. And, like most boys who were later to write about their childhood, Marcel is also an admirer of Robinson Crusoe ('un de mes héros favoris', *Château*, p.88). Defoe's Robinson survived by stamping his personality on his surroundings, refashioning his new unfamiliar world with himself as its centre and turning the island into an extension of his desires. Marcel automatically assumes that he is the centre of the universe and views himself as just such a castaway. He revels in the insularity of his imagination. He borrows Robinson's resourcefulness and ingenuity to transform everyday reality into exotic adventure. The repair of the broken furniture bought by Joseph is effected with a home-made tool 'digne de Robinson Crusoé' (*Gloire*, p.66) and he uses Robinson's example to convince himself that he will grow into a satisfactory 'Hermite des collines' who will master his environment and live off the land (*Château*, p.70). But he is even more excited by the tales of Fenimore Cooper (1789-1851) and the now forgotten Gustave Aymard (1818-83) which he wraps cosily round himself. He becomes a Red Indian and peoples the hills with grizzly bears, pumas, lions and boa-constrictors. He turns uncle Jules into Buffalo Bill, but takes most satisfaction from the fact that he is the great hunter's nephew. Pagnol gives Marcel's imagination a distinctly literary turn which insulates him from the real world and imparts the throb of heightened vitality to banal events.

Marcel acquires several literary identities and lives up to all of them. He is not only Robinson but a trapper, a tracker and an Indian brave who prefers the hatchet of war to the pipe of peace. He invests his surroundings and everyday objects with an aura of adventure derived from ripping yarns which are much more exciting than ordinary life. He turns the hills into trackless jungles, practises with an 'authentic' Indian bow and changes a sparrow-hawk into a condor (*Gloire*, p.184). He has complete faith in book-lore. When he is lost, he lopes along with the classic 'trot indien' which he has read about, sucks a pebble to slake his thirst in the approved manner, seeks his bearings by the sun, rubs sticks together to start a fire, smears herbs on his legs to heal the scratches, thinks of lighting a signal beacon and is wary of abandoned cabins which are invariably used by

murderous Indians who lie in wait for the unsuspecting traveller, a
danger familiar to anyone who lives on the prairie. His concept of
the 'hermit's life' is similarly derived from the 'vingtaines de livres'
he has read, and when committed to attacking the 'grisibou' he
wonders what Robinson would have done (*Château*, pp.69-70, 88).
Marcel consciously bases his own conduct upon that of his heroes.
Jules says hunters eat a lot, so Marcel asks for second helpings
(*Gloire*, p.161). He chokes back sobs 'que le Coeur Loyal eût blamés'
(*ib.*, p.188). When he is at a loss for what to do, he simply plays at
being somebody else, for while he is totally committed to each of the
roles he adopts, he moves easily between them. Lost on the
mountainside, 'J'abandonnai donc mon rôle de trappeur, et mon
astuce de Comanche, et j'eus aussitôt la courageuse patience de
Robinson' (*ib.*, p.193).

Marcel plays many such self-aggrandising parts, from trapper,
'héros accablé' and 'hermite des collines' to the 'penseur' he appears
to be at school and the 'gentleman' Lili sees in him. All his roles have
'une réalité obsédante' (*Gloire*, p.111) because the power of his
imagination makes reality seem dull in comparison. But if Marcel's
mind gives fantastic shapes to what is, Pagnol also shows that he
learns to transform what has been. When he recounts his part in the
affair of the 'bartavelles', his tale fails to make an impact; so, for the
benefit of his mother and Paul he turns it into a 'récit pathétique' (*ib.*,
p.201). When he and Lili escape the 'grand-duc' and find their way
home through the fog, Marcel is delighted with an adventure which
promises 'de beaux récits' which he duly tells with such success that
he gives himself bad dreams and, later, regrets 'les descriptions que
j'en avais faites' (*Château*, pp.48, 50, 87). Marcel does not merely
live his fantasies. He becomes a story-teller.

But the world of books and knowledge cannot overcome
reality. The survival tips he remembers from books do not work: the
herbs he puts on his scratches only make them hurt more and he
never does find out which way is East. It also dawns on him that Lili,
who has much less imagination and far more real knowledge, is the
'vrai Comanche' (*Château*, p.16): he knows instinctively that
Robinson is a 'beau menteur' (*ib.*, p.70). Marcel talks him down

using the adult argument that 'c'est imprimé, dans un livre qu'on donne pour les prix'. But Lili's belief in ghosts is stronger than the magic of Joseph's disbelief which Marcel intones desperately (*ib.*, p.83). Books and book-learning, which initially helped to make the world comprehensible, exciting and manageable, prove to be a disappointment: life cannot be remade to fit the shape of our desires.

v) Marcel and Imagination

Marcel's literary fantasies are only one aspect of the ways his vivid imagination poeticises reality. In the wind that whistles around Chantepierre, a finger of rock on the summit of Tête-Rouge, he sees graceful visions of lords and ladies — though Lili, whose ear is 'aveugle', hears nothing (*Château*, p.29). Most of the time, however, his imagination acts as a form of optimism by removing the stages between a thought and its realisation. It takes very little for Marcel to jump from what is to what might be. Joseph has only to announce the construction of the new tram-line for Marcel to see rails sprout in the grass and hear the rumble of non-existent trams; if his father speaks of the Evils of Drink, he expects the removal man to drop dead instantly (*Gloire*, pp.81, 95); Jules's coat of many pockets is a virtual guarantee of an abundance of game (*ib.*, p.155). He wonders what it would be like to break a leg (*Château*, p.63) but decides instead to live in a cave: his plans are immediately translated into a vision of himself as a self-sufficient hermit, hair blowing, hands in pockets, with a talking starling on his shoulder (*ib.*, pp.71-72). His waking imagination is different from his dreams only insofar as his dreams are even more surrealistic: a giant hare carries him off to slumberland (*Gloire*, p.204); he kills the caretaker in the most dramatic manner (*Château*, p.155); and, after Bouzigue's tale of his sister, a confused nightmare reveals just how little he has understood of grown-up realities (*ib.*, p.213).

But though the distortions of imagination are powerful, they do not last, and Marcel is insulated against disappointment by new fancies and impressions which quickly displace them: the name of Raspagnetto, hailed as a saviour one day, is forgotten the next

(*Château*, pp.198, 200). Imagination is a shield, for once he is launched on some inner adventure, it removes the need to consider anyone's feelings but his own. He callously dismisses the sufferings of the praying mantis: 'La colique des tigres,' he declares, 'je m'en fous' (*Gloire*, p.109). He considers Paul to be an infant and, playing the role of elder brother, looks after him, tucking him up in bed and making up a pack for him to carry (*Gloire*, p.51, *Château*, p.116). Yet he has difficulty in recognising Paul's separateness and usually sees him in relation to himself: feeling guilty for abandoning him and 'imaginant sa solitude', he takes him hunting but fails to sense that Paul would much prefer to stay with 'la petite soeur' (*Château*, pp.31-32).

Of course, Pagnol exploits the power of Marcel's imagination for comic purposes, but he also shows that his games of make-believe are an important part of the process of growing up. In this sense, the *Souvenirs d'enfance* offer a number of shrewd insights and reflections upon the way in which children acquire what we call an 'identity'. The roles Marcel plays allow him to experience real emotions within the safe bounds of unreality. He knows fear when pursued by the 'condor', despair when he is lost, and horror in the tale of the 'tripes de Malbousquet'. His fantasies are exercises in 'muscle-flexing' which will prepare him to face adult realities. By living in a world of play and make-believe, he multiplies his personality and tries out different personas as a means of defining who he is. Some of the qualities of his models rub off on him and Pagnol notes: 'c'est parfois en jouant le héros qu'un cabotin devient un héros véritable' (*Château*, p.170). On the other hand, he later doubted if he had ever chosen to be any one of them: 'Quand je revois la longue série de personnages que j'ai joués dans ma vie, je me demande qui je suis' (*Amours*, p.7).

Though Marcel occasionally frightens himself with the wild beasts and dangers he invents, his imagination generally acts as a powerful defence mechanism. It is a source of reassurance: there is safety in his fantasies. He copes with reality more easily as Robinson or a Comanche than as himself. They are not simply roles to play but role models to follow, and he consciously bases his conduct on them.

Confronted by the 'grosibou', he finds the courage he lacks in their example: if he turned and ran, 'je n'aurais plus le droit d'entrer dans un roman d'aventures, et les personnages des illustrations, qui m'avaient toujours regardé en face, détourneraient la tête pour ne pas voir un "coeur de squaw"' (*Château*, p.89). At such moments, we may observe how Marcel's personality begins to acquire consistency through his budding awareness of the approval and disapproval of others.

But Pagnol casts grave doubts upon the usefulness of Marcel's literary lore which, in any case, next to Lili's practical knowledge, is artificial and self-deceiving. It stimulates his vanity and leads him to believe that the clichés he has found in books and heard from Joseph can be used to impose order upon chaos. In reality, literary intelligence will be as unsatisfactory as academic success in helping him to understand the world. His very first experience of reading, when he deciphers Joseph's blackboard sentence about the mother who punished the naughty boy, is misleading. But reading too many books does not merely lead to a false view of reality: it is ultimately self-defeating. Later, he discovers Jules Verne and the older Pagnol notes sadly that 'ses inventions remplaçaient la féerie perdue de mes collines' (*Secrets*, p.23). Paradoxically, the yarns which once helped him master the incomprehensible world now banish it completely and in the process destroy the magic of natural ignorance.

Pagnol describes the mechanism of the child's imagination vividly and holds it up as a crucial source of wonder. But he also shows the forces which threaten it. When Marcel sees gunpowder, which looks like ground charcoal, he finds it dull compared to the picture he had formed of it in his mind (*Gloire*, pp.139-40). When the family sets off to spend a chilly Christmas at Les Bellons, he is delighted with his warm clothes which make him feel, romantically, like a seal-hunter. 'La beauté de cet équipement me ravit: mais je découvris par la suite ses inconvénients. Il y avait tant de boutons, de crochets, de brides et d'épingles de sûreté que le grand problème, c'était de faire pipi proprement' (*Château*, p.115). The 'formidable' Marcel finds it difficult to sustain the role he plays: 'On a beau être formidable, il y a des moments où le destin nous trahit' (*Château*, p.87). Imagination is a fine thing, but reality keeps breaking through.

vi) Marcel: Sensation, Magic and Reason

Marcel's earliest memories — of his grandfather's curly hair, black eyes and childlike laugh, the slaughter of animals in the abattoir or the accidents which befall cyclists in the park — are vivid because they are rooted in sensation. Like the torture of the 'pregadiou', they are detached from moral sense. The external world is a form of theatre staged for his amusement, a spectacle full of interesting happenings. He is a privileged observer who has no responsibility for his actions and reactions. Nature is even more of a 'fairyland' than the second-hand furniture shop and, as we have seen, Marcel becomes aware of it through his senses. Pagnol makes much of Marcel's sensual awareness. He recalls the feel of things, the taste of food and above all smells which he distinguishes very acutely: 'parfums' are muted by the early-morning dew (*Château*, p.79) while at other times 'parfums' turn into 'odeurs' (*ib.*, p.40) which reassure, like the 'vieille odeur de la bergerie' where he and Lili shelter (*ib.*, p.48). Some smells exist in his imagination, like the 'lavandes perdues' he dreams of (*ib.*, p.134) or the 'odeur ancienne de rôti' he detects in Sleeping Beauty's castle (*ib.*, pp.164-65). But his world is also filled with sound: the noise of the storm gives way to gentle rain in which 'tous les bruits étaient amortis' (*ib.*, p.98), and he is struck particularly by 'le silence glacé' which makes La Bastide so different in winter (*ib.*, p.129).

Marcel, then, lives in a world of sensation which makes reality seem dull. Games in the school playground are 'rapetissés and désenchantés' when he thinks of the adventures to come (*Gloire*, p.72). Adult conversation, normally tedious, becomes 'absolument féerique' when its subject is hunting (*ib.*, p.74). The removal waggon turns into 'le chariot de l'aventure et de l'espoir' and François becomes 'le messager des vacances' and an 'empereur romain', while the tram — 'ô merveille!' — goes faster than a horse and makes Marcel feel that he is the 'vainqueur de l'espace et du temps' (*ib.*, pp.74-76). But he gradually learns that not all sensations are as pleasant and that he cannot always control the circumstances in which they originate. He feels protective towards Augustine and does what he can for her, but he is unable to make her less frail. On the other hand, he can overcome his vulnerability to lesser difficulties by using a variety of techniques. We have seen how he shelters behind bookish personas and retreats into his imagination when he feels threatened. But he also resorts to superstition as a means of coping with circumstances which are new or strange or menacing. Before the holidays start, he repeats 'quelques mots magiques' like 'villa' and 'cigales' in a ritual of anticipation (*ib.*, p.72). When he is lost he recites one of Joseph's dictums to give himself strength: he knows no 'fervent prayers' but a 'formule magique' is a secular substitute (*ib.*, p.195). Confronted with the possibility that ghosts exist, philosophical truths prove less reassuring than the sign of the cross (*Château*, pp.83-85). He swears an oath of secrecy with Lili (*ib.*, p.41) and irrationally regards a snare as a 'sacred relic' of friendship (*ib.*, p.100). By resorting to magical practices, Marcel is able to control the world he lives in and the fears it starts.

He enjoys the sensation of fear, especially when it is induced by imagination — but only as long as he knows that he is safe: each day's danger ends at bedtime. But until he is called in for supper, he comes to terms with it as best he can. Magic is one weapon but more important is reason. He is always trying to make sense of what goes on, though he does not always draw the right conclusions. Pagnol makes much of his childish misunderstandings. Marcel speculates wildly about how babies are born and in the political talk of the grown-ups sees a haze of warring gangs of 'framassons' and 'tartruffes' (*Gloire*, p. 114). He reasons that Jules, who is a heaven-bound Catholic, won't mind dying as much as Joseph, who is not (*ib.*, p. 172), and the story of Trinquette Edouard leads him to the conclusion ('assez peu rationnelle') that God exists for some people but not for others (*Château*, p.127). He wonders whether birds have patois of their own (*ib.*, p.72) and is easily misled by appearances: the count looks villainous but is kind (*ib.*, pp.158-59) and the caretaker who looks like a murderer is good-hearted (*ib.*, p.167). But if logic leads him astray, reason also saves him. After losing contact with Joseph and Jules, he defuses his panic and rejoins them as much by judgment as luck. But Marcel also uses reason as a means of manipulating others. His 'misreading' of Lamennais's fable (left to his devices he would give the grapes to his mother but would eat half of them first) (*Gloire*, p.119) is an early indication of how selfish he is. There are many instances of his deviousness and opportunism in furthering his own interest which confirm Pagnol's general contention that reason 'ne sert le plus souvent qu'à justifier nos croyances' (*ib.*, p.16). As he grows older, the habit of expediency looks set to undermine the need for magic as a way of avoiding unpleasant sensations and preferring what he finds agreeable. It is one more step in the loss of his innocence.

vii) Marcel and Language.

Among Marcel's earliest memories are the words he reads on Joseph's blackboard. Thereafter, his struggles with language continue to play a crucial part in his development. He battles with the political vocabulary used by Joseph and Jules, mishandles the word 'secondaire' and the mysterious jargon of school (*Château*, pp.102, 170-71) and wildly misinterprets Bouzigue's account of his sister's 'left-handed' marriage (*ib.*, pp.138, 212-13). He tries out grown-up words and makes serious efforts to behave to the standards of maturity that they assume: thus he 'rehearses' his death at the stake (*Gloire*, p.124), borrows Joseph's aphorisms and trusts to the magical properties of expressions found in books: he knows that rescuers will come with torches made 'de bois résineux' (*ib.*, p.194) and makes himself drunk on the exotic tarantulas and vampires which exist in his reading and not in his experience. The issue is important to him since labelling things is a means of mastering them. His father's old gun is a source of shame, but as 'un souvenir de famille' it is eminently respectable (*ib.*, p.135). His knife is reassuring when he thinks of it as a 'machète'. He finds or borrows labels for his father which fix his hunting exploit in linguistic amber: Joseph is 'le vainqueur' returned from an 'odyssée', the 'Tueur de Bartavelles' and a 'grand fusil' (*ib.*, pp.199, 200, 208). Words authenticate experience and Marcel's experience of words is an essential part of the learning process: language is power.

He collects words as other boys collect stamps, but his 'passion' for their sounds and 'belles images' (*Gloire*, p.115) cannot remain pure. Words are in the front line of his battle with his surroundings. The expression 'nous coller les boyaux' throws him into a panic (*ib.*, p.104). 'Poudre' may lose its charm but 'superstition', 'obscurantise' (*sic*) and 'pantomime' are useful allies against fear (*Château*, pp.84-85) — but not as useful as 'glapir', a verb he had often carried around in his school bag, which removes the threat from the bark of the fox (*ib.*, p.81).

Marcel's first experience of the world is linguistic but the words he uses have private meanings and talismanic properties which enhance reality yet do not always reflect it accurately. But Pagnol follows Marcel far enough for it to be clear that the further his language skills develop, the better he is able to master himself and his surroundings. But in the process, the magic is mislaid as the sound and shape of words are refilled by commonly agreed meanings. It will never be recaptured.

viii) Marcel and Other People

'Comme presque tous les enfants,' Manon, daughter of Jean de Florette, 'ne savait à peu près rien de la vie passée de ses parents' (*Manon des sources*, Livre de Poche, p.287). Pagnol knows as little as Manon about his parents and his account of his birth has the ring of literary invention. It is significant, however, that while he explores Joseph's education (albeit in general terms), he makes no attempt to look into his mother's past. Joseph was always a grown-up but Marcel silently assumes that Augustine and he were born on the same day. If Joseph grows older and maintains his twenty-five year lead, Augustine remained eternally nineteen in Pagnol's memory (*Gloire*, p.22). Pagnol's 'filial piety' is directed mainly at his mother.

She is a shadowy figure and Pagnol evokes her with protective tenderness. Joseph explains that she needs country air (*Gloire*, p.55) but no details are given of her illness. Yet the adjectives used to describe her — 'pâle', 'frêle', 'timide', 'petite', 'menue', 'bien mince' (or 'pas bien épaisse' as Bouzigue puts it) — give an impression of fragility. Sometimes, 'jeune et belle' in her summer holiday clothes, she looks no more than a pink-cheeked fifteen (*ib.*, pp.74, 90) while, dressed for winter, with colour again in her cheeks, she 'ressemblait aux belles patineuses canadiennes qui glissaient sur le calendrier des postes' (*Château*, p.116). Yet the trek to Les Bellons leaves her 'exténuée' and Marcel is struck by 'la pâleur de ses yeux cernés'. Fear of discovery produces the same result: 'La pâleur muette de ma mère me serrait le coeur' (*Château*, p.180). Augustine is a frail figure, delicate as a bird.

She is 'sûre de son Joseph' (*Gloire*, p.143) and 'capable de tout' for the good of her children: she has 'le Génie de l'Intrigue' (*Château*, pp.131, 133). She lacks Joseph's education and Pagnol occasionally mocks her narrow horizons: she fears that reading will injure Marcel's brain, imagines microbes to be like tigers, and believes naïvely that wealth is the just reward for hard work and academic success (*Gloire*, pp.32-33, 58; *Château*, p.53). But most of the time she is seen through Marcel's uncritical eyes. He is tenderly attentive: he pretends to have a pain in his ankle to give her a few moments' rest, fetches shoes which are easier for her to walk in and is even prepared to risk his life by shielding her from the blast when Joseph's gun is tested. Yet as he grows older, so he grows away from her. To persuade his parents to stay, he ignobly uses her frailty as a blackmailing excuse and says that town is bad for her health (*Château*, pp.54-55). His love of the hills is stronger than his love for Augustine. 'Je la regardais avec tendresse, mais j'étais parfaitement décidé à la quitter la nuit suivante' (*ib.*, p.73). He peels the potatoes as a 'geste d'amour' and blows a kiss to her alone, but he goes all the same. The ties that bind him to her are loosened, though her death later brought them close once more. Augustine plays a minor role in Pagnol's recollections but she holds the moral centre. Her memory inspires a moment of genuine grief and Pagnol, normally an easy-going man, is moved to anger as he smashes the gate of 'le Père Humilié'. But if his father is avenged, the shade of his eternally 'inconsolable' mother walks the path: she will never know that 'elle était chez son fils'. It is as much as Pagnol ever revealed of his true feelings.

On the other hand, Joseph plays a more prominent role and is much more fully drawn. Pagnol describes his physical appearance in detail (*Gloire*, p.21) and shows him to be a heavily pedantic man marked by the 'ineradicable lessons' of the Collège Normal where he trained. He has views on everything. Society is 'absurd' because the Republic tolerates private property (*ib.*, pp.78-79). He denounces religion as obscurantist superstition and regards the sentimental morality of Lamennais as a conspiracy designed by the ruling class to keep the people docile and submissive (*ib.*, p.120). In his view, aristocrats ('des gens insolents et cruels') are still the oppressors of the people (*ib.*, p.115). But violence and Revolution are no solution to society's injustice: 'l'horreur des grands massacres enlaidit jusqu'aux victimes' (*Château*, p.141). It is his duty to warn of the dangers of drink and he does so. Having been taught that ignorance is the prime cause of the misery of the people, he sprays his variegated knowledge in all directions. He gives lectures about lizards and donkeys (*ib.*, pp.77, 86), informs Marcel that the boa eats only once a month (*Château*, p.61) and enthusiastically communicates the fruits of his researches into the geology and rainfall of the area (*ib.*, p.20). But though primarily a teacher and a books man, he never wastes an opportunity to learn. He inquires of François the etymology of Taoumé and Toubé and is interested by the origin of the word 'bartavelle' supplied by the curé (*Gloire*, pp.88, 211). He is eager to be taught about hunting by Jules and equips himself for his role as unofficial canal inspector by reading up on the subject (*Château*, p.152). His respect for 'l'Université', that is the whole educational system, ensures that he is never off duty. A relentlessly 'grand pédagogue, c'est-à-dire doreur de pilules' (*Gloire*, p.110), he slips lessons into everything. Thus the ant is 'le modèle du bon citoyen' while the praying mantis is an accurate image for the rapacity of the church (*ib.*, pp.104, 106). He positively drools at the prospect of turning bullet-making into a rich source of arithmetical problems (*ib.*, p.141) and sees 'une valeur éducative dans toutes les catastrophes' (*ib.*, p.132): thus he uses an enforced stop to warn of the perils of sheltering under trees in a storm (*Château*, pp.35-36).

But Joseph is not a bore. He plays boules, draughts and the flute and has a great capacity for fun. He makes a noise like a trumpet to wake Marcel and pretends to be a horse when they set out to buy the furniture (*Gloire*, pp.53, 61). He makes jokes about roads that go up then down, about Herod's combinations and about walking between the raindrops to avoid getting wet (*ib.*, pp.60, 62, 113). He uses his 'invention géniale' to turn washing into a game (*ib.*, p.103). He makes even dull things interesting: he finds ways of making Paul feel important by telling him that unless they are watched his tools will hide (*ib.*, p.67). His passion for pottering and for making useless objects releases his imagination and inventiveness (*ib.*, pp.58-59) and at times he seems hardly older than his own children: when he tells Marcel, ironically, that he too would like to live in a cave, the reader can quite believe it (*Château*, p.99).

This portrait of Joseph, with his 'omniscience paternelle' and sense of fun, is like the pictures small children draw from knee-height of grown-ups whose legs, foreshortened, spring directly out of their necks. But as time passes, the monolithic Joseph is cut down to size in Marcel's mind. Pagnol's caricaturing of his ideas and pedagogical obsessions prepares us for the contradictions which Marcel gradually perceives in him. Marcel wonders why the President of France does not call him in to sort out the nation's problems (*Gloire*, p.79), though we can see why. Joseph may be fearless in words but he is in practice intimidated by authority: the word of the school *concierge* commands respect (*ib.*, p.34), while his misgivings about the short-cut across private property are motivated by fear of law-breaking. Nor does he practise what he preaches: his views on the dangers of vanity are contradicted by his lap of honour with the 'bartavelles', showing them to Mond ('pour s'instruire') and allowing the arch-enemy the curé to take his photograph which he examines at length on the specious ground that 'photography' interests him. Indeed, the moment is full of contradictions. Joseph the pacifist kills, with a 'coup du roi', birds which are admired by the Church, and thus sells out his anti-militarist, anti-royalist and anti-clerical principles in an orgy of self-congratulation. But Marcel is still young enough to be dazzled and does not love his father any less. All the same Joseph is caught 'en flagrant délit d'humanité' and Marcel is given a real intimation that Joseph is not perfect but has feet of clay. Marcel's shame about Joseph's old gun evaporates quickly and his earlier doubts about Joseph's 'toute-puissance' (*ib.*, pp.134, 153) had been swept away by his amazing hunting exploit: he did not 'rentrer bredouille' (*ib.*, p.176) after all, but returned a hero. But after the 'bartavelles', Joseph never quite recovers his omnipotence in Marcel's eyes. He is wrong about mulled wine, not necessarily correct about ghosts, wide of the mark in his view of aristocrats — the comte is charming — and, though a socialist, he owns shares in rail-ways (*Château*, pp.123, 83, 160-61, 199). The taller Marcel grows, the less he finds to look up to.

But Joseph's shortcomings are seen most clearly in his inability to deal with awkward realities. He is quite unable to handle the discrepancy between his views on alcohol and the obligations of politeness: he mixes wine and mineral water and calls it foolishly 'une sorte de champagne', and takes a sip of brandy on the understanding that he does so for 'medicinal purposes' (*Château*, pp.146, 194). He may emerge from the furniture shop with 'bargains', but he has been forced to pay more than he intended. It is Bouzigue, a former pupil, who teaches him lessons which he is incapable of learning. Joseph is prepared to put up with his 'peine': Bouzigue automatically looks for the easy way. Joseph hates influence on principle: Bouzigue uses his shameless sister shamelessly to further his interests. Joseph the etymologist cannot distinguish between a 'danger' and a 'catastrophe' and has a rigid view of legality: Bouzigue, a more practical spirit, brushes aside such linguistic diffi- culties and simply manipulates 'le règlement'. Even Joseph's political views take a beating. He admires the 'patriotic' stance of the keeper of the third castle: Bouzigue dismisses it by saying the old man is in his dotage. Joseph's anti-militarism is dented when he realises that the colonel is a Warrior Hero who, furthermore, proceeds to 'ennoble' the Pagnols' republican house with the 'roses du roy' he gives to Augustine. When Joseph faces the bullying caretaker, he trails no glory — 'Il fut sincère et pathétique, mais piteux' (*ib.*, p.185) — and it is left to Bouzigue to retrieve the situation.

Just as Marcel gradually learns to bring reality to heel through make-believe, imagination and language, so Joseph possesses the world through education. He believes that knowledge is power, and within the classroom and the family, knowledge serves him well, for he is a good teacher and a contented man. He can only accept Bouzigue's key by rationalising his role: as an unpaid 'expert', his reason allows him to do what he fears to do. But generally he is too upright to take short-cuts of any kind and in worldly terms is doomed to be a failure, for he never learns. The last words we hear him speak express his outrage that 'en ce monde, le vice soit trop souvent récompensé' (*Château*, p.213). Waking from his dream in which Joseph has been annihilated by the forces which got the better of him in real life, Marcel — with Pagnol's full support — shares the exasperation of Bouzigue at the impracticability of his views which remain general and intellectual to the end. Joseph, who began as a hero, ends as a disappointment.

None of the other figures in Marcel's world touch him as nearly as Augustine, who is beyond criticism, and Joseph, whose stock falls steadily. Of the adults, Rose is lightly sketched as part of the reassuring background. Pagnol tells us that she is naïve enough to think herself 'une véritable courtisane' for meeting a man in the park. She is also prudish enough to rechristen him Jules and too innocent to know that 'Jules' is also a name for a chamber-pot. Marcel simply knows her as a cosy aunt, who fusses over Pierre and cannot live without Gas. Jules, on the other hand, is much more clearly drawn. He provides a sharp contrast with Joseph. He is a better-paid civil servant, has a small private income and seems almost a foreigner to Marcel. He hails from the Roussillon and rolls his r's as though suffering from 'une infirmité cachée' (*Gloire*, p.44) which allows him to give the word 'bartavelle' a magical ring (*ib.*, p.129). As a right-wing Catholic, he is the perfect foil for Joseph though the two men are bound by a 'vraie amitié' (*Château*, p.125).

He is pompous (Jules 'se flattait d'être un organisateur', *Gloire*, p.73) and he enjoys his authority over Joseph in the matter of testing guns, making bullets and hunting, for then he becomes a 'savant' and 'professeur' instructing an 'élève' and 'apprenti' (*ib.*, p.142). Jules's superiority gives Marcel his first doubts about his father's omnipotence, yet he is fascinated by this splendid uncle who is fond of jokes (how to get a good shot at a boar using truffles, *ib.*, pp.131-32) but fonder still of blood-thirsty hunting stories, like the tale of the 'tripes de Malbousquet' or the unfortunate death of M. Bénazet (*ib.*, pp.131, 137) — not to mention accounts of his own exploits which he punctuates with 'et que vois-je?' He is larger than life: he is the 'owner' of the park, of a magical hunting coat, of a new rifle. But he is also a representative of the grown-up world which does not always play fair: he pretends that Marcel is not one of the children to whom it is permissible to lie — and then sneakily excludes him from the hunting party. He also encourages him to work hard for his exams, and speaks in glowing terms of Latin (*Château*, p.53). Jules is an unassailable member of the unassailable adult male clan — until Rose, who rules him firmly, finds reasons for staying at home with the Gas. Jules's absence from the tale after Christmas 1904 reveals to Marcel that even great hunters cannot do what they wish.

Marcel's sister is so beneath his notice that she is never named, while his cousin Pierre, a 'pompeur de biberons', is despised and disliked when he starts being a rival for the family's attention (*Château*, p.113). Paul, however, has a definite personality which develops as time passes. Apart from being 'voracious', his major characteristic is a kind of disinterested cruelty which co-exists with a genuine sensitivity. He tortures anything he can lay his hands on: lizards, ants, grasshoppers, even his sister. Yet he has a horror of suffering and kindheartedly tries to reassemble the dismembered 'pregadiou' (*Gloire*, p.106). He angrily demands immediate punishment for François who beats the mule (*ib.*, p.84) and devises a scheme for stabbing the castle caretaker to death: 'je le tue dans les fesses' (*Château*, p.154). He finds the 'tripes de Malbousquet' especially funny (*Gloire*, p.131), but when he begins to read storybooks, his imagination, like Marcel's, acquires a fanciful turn

(*Château*, p.154). He too is fascinated by words and Pagnol uses his passing whim for 'passoire' as an effective running joke. But Paul is temperamentally hostile to hunting: 'il faut le démourir', he demands, when he is shown a dead finch in a snare (*ib.*, p.32). He prefers not to wander far from the house and is not upset for long by the prospect of the return to school (*Gloire*, pp.58-59). Paul is young and still sees the world as a spectacle designed for his amusement. Marcel has grown out of this stage and Paul's childishness is a constant reminder of another role that he plays, that of older brother. He is capable of feeling a 'honteuse jalousie' when Paul rides on the mule (*ib.*, p.81), but most of the time he protects him, sometimes unnecessarily. Paul makes him feel older than his years and Marcel, taking a leaf out of Joseph's book, uses the bait of a humming-bird or the threat of soap and water to get rid of him when he is not wanted. Marcel feels superior enough to lie to him 'for his own good'. Paul, a force of nature, cannot be wished away, and coping with the permanent fact of his existence is an important factor in shaping Marcel's growing sense of self-identity.

But Marcel is not significantly disturbed in his insulated world until Lili appears in his life. Lili does not have his imagination, has not read books, does not know many long words (he says 'micropes' for 'microbes') and cannot spell. Marcel shows off shamelessly: he speaks of exotic lands and dangerous creatures and learns his thirteen-times table to impress him. But from the moment they meet, he senses that Lili does not play games but lives in the real world. He knows real Provençal words for real Provençal things and speaks authoritatively of plants and birds, of country lore and the weather which he understands better than Jules. He applies his 'esprit pratique' to Marcel's wild plans for retiring to his cave: he promises real provisions and suggests a practical livelihood. Marcel tries to beat him into submission with his superior education and a selection of Joseph's aphorisms, but Lili knows that Robinson Crusoe is a liar and that ghosts do exist. Marcel senses that Lili is the 'vrai Comanche' and is forced to recognise that it is he who is 'formidable' (*Château*, pp. 16, 88). But Lili does not simply puncture Marcel's make-believe world and give him a sense of reality. He also arouses genuine feelings of a new kind. Until Marcel meets Lili, he is rarely self-critical. But the way he abandons his scheme to live in the hills fills him with shame: 'J'avais menti à mes parents, j'avais menti à mon ami, je m'étais menti à moi-même' (*ib*., pp.95-96). He has abused Lili's friendship and traded on his trusting nature, and he does not like the feeling. When Lili writes, Marcel senses the 'coeur' and the 'vraie délicatesse' which Joseph also notes. But when he comes to reply, he abandons his plan to show off and adds spelling mistakes and the blot which shines like the sun of true friendship. Lili continues to stand in awe of of Marcel the 'gentleman', but Marcel has learned to respect him as an equal. Which is why he knows the value of the untruth Lili tells about waiting for Durbec: it is the lie of a friend (*ib*., p.121). Later that summer, as Pagnol relates in *Le Temps des secrets*, Marcel deserts Lili for Isabelle before resuming their adventures on a more modest scale. But as his inclusion in the trinity of Pagnol's coda suggests, the lesson he learnt from Lili was never forgotten.

Unlike the objects in Marcel's world, the people around him cannot be imagined away. The adults impose a framework of rules upon him which define his place in the hierarchy. But whether friends or foes, all represent opposition to his will, for all have desires which have to be placated. Marcel's increasingly sophisticated relationships force him to give a response to what exists outside him. People lay siege to the castle of his autonomous imagination. It is only a matter of time before the walls are breached and finally levelled.

ix) Marcel and Moral Values

The people who at first stand on the edges of Marcel's world steadily creep forward into his consciousness and help give a shape to his personality and a direction to his values. In this sense, his childhood is very much a learning process and Pagnol carefully charts the growth of Marcel's moral being.

At the outset, external reality is a series of peculiar images and the world full of giants who quarrel about a piece of string (*Gloire*, p.29). Suffering is a source of entertainment for Marcel who discovers that he can influence his surroundings in a variety of ways — he can make ducks run away by throwing stones at them and can placate parental demands by making a suitable show of obedience: his sound effects become an effective substitute for washing. Marcel contracts a habit of deviousness at an early age. When he wants to stay up to watch Jules make bullets, he plays on his father's obsession with education by claiming it will be a useful 'object lesson' (*ib.*, p.134). He does not dare ask if the grown-ups will take him out on the first day of the season, and raises the question obliquely: perhaps they need a retriever (*ib.*, pp.145-46)? He uses every piece of special pleading he can think of in his efforts to persuade the family to stay at La Bastide Neuve, even stooping to using Augustine's health as an excuse (*Château*, pp.55-64). But he is never more than a small-time hypocrite and his sensitivity saves him from extremes of egoism. Even as he tricks Lili with tales of 'micropes', he is painfully aware of his 'mauvaise foi ignoble' (*ib.*, p.93).

His deviousness is part of the wider problem of lying. At first, Marcel believes that reality is precisely what it appears to be. But when he learns that Jules does not own the park, he is both reassured and disconcerted. The 'imposture' justifies 'mes propres mensonges passés, présents et futurs' but he knows now that he cannot always trust other people, for they too tell lies (*Gloire*, p.47). Jules in particular is associated with lying. His indirect manner of extracting information about game from local people infringes Joseph's principles of honesty (*ib.*, p.126) and by allowing Marcel to believe he is not a child who needs to be lied to 'for his own good', Jules confirms Marcel's indignant suspicion that grown-ups do not play the game (*ib.*, pp.161-64). Marcel, who does not believe in playing games he cannot win (*ib.*, p.143), learns to keep a sharper eye open — and with it detects subtler departures from truth. Thus he perceives Joseph's pride as fêted hunter as part of his humanity: it is unconscious and understandable in a way that his own 'cabotinage' at school is not. He recognises Lili's fabrication for what it is: a 'friendship lie'. Marcel learns to pick his way through the mists of untruth and misleading appearances.

Experience is thus his teacher. By using tools, he becomes aware of the 'prodigieuse efficacité' of his hands (*Gloire*, p.69). When put to the test, he shields Augustine instinctively against exploding guns, with no thought for his own safety: he does not need Lamennais's sentimental guidance to help him love his mother. Impressions that stick in his mind contradict or confirm later lessons: the memory of the white-owl which tore its own head off undermines the reputation of Minerva as the goddess of wisdom, while a phrase of Baudelaire later acquires meaning when he recalls the face of the castle caretaker (*Château*, pp.27, 188). Experience teaches him that even adults who tell lies (like Jules) are not free to do as they wish (*ib*., p.114) though it also shows him that honesty and a respect for truth do not help his upright father to deal with life on life's terms. Joseph is not weak because he is wrong but because he is 'pure' (*ib*., p.191). But this is a lesson which Pagnol admits acquiring only later in life and Marcel, who has learned much, has yet to learn how to behave. He still likes playing to win, as his rivalry with Oliva indicates, and he has been introduced to friendship. But he has begun to judge adults who cease to be giants. He continues to act out roles, but knows that others do so too. He has learned that loyalties change and moral choices are difficult. He has not found the secret of living, but he has made a start.

Although Pagnol describes himself as a 'mémorialiste', the *Souvenirs d'enfance* are not 'memoirs' in the sense used by Georges May (see above, p.17). He does not set out to chronicle an age but to rediscover the flavour of a self which once was his and to reflect upon it. He inserts himself into Marcel's skin and explores the growth of his psychology. The biographical data given in chapter 2 furnish a more factual account of his childhood. But a biography, which is a life seen from the outside, is very different from an autobiographical 'Childhood', which is an early life remembered from within. Pagnol's relative lack of interest in the documentary aspects of his past clearly emphasises his priorities: the loss of innocence and the emergence of his conscious self. His focus remains constantly on Marcel as though to underline his general contention that nothing exists which Marcel does not see or imagine. Pagnol's truth is human truth and his concern is as much with moral issues as with psychology. Yet what he writes has a strong narrative drive, a formal structure and characters as memorable as those which people his plays and films. Pagnol's autobiographical purpose is quite clear. But to what extent is it shaped by Pagnol the literary artist?

4. Pagnol and the Temptation of Literature

The past is an unreal place governed by operations of selective memory more powerful than logic, the dictates of time and the laws of the physical universe. Primeval excitements survive like mountains which tower above flatlands of routine and dull habit. The geography of Pagnol's childhood is ordered according to just such eccentric principles.

As a map of his past, *La Gloire de mon père* is suitably distorted. A section on his ancestors and birth (pp.11-29) is followed by an account of his first memories which take quickly him to 1903 when he is eight (pp.30-53). The rest of the volume covers a period of a few months, from April to the middle of August of a year which, as we have seen, is two years silently combined. Pages 54-98 deal with the preparations for the family's *transhumance* to the moment of installation at the end of July. Pagnol dwells briefly on his first impressions of his exciting new environment (pp.99-121) before moving to the preparations for the hunt (pp.122-53) which unfolds dramatically (pp.154-98) and ends with the return and the tour of triumph (pp.199-214). The brief documentary section (to p.29) is followed by impressionistic recollections (to p.53), while the rest of the volume (160 pages in all) follows a very clearly defined narrative thrust, occupying a few months and building to a dramatic climax. Clearly, the bulk of *La Gloire de mon père* is told like a story.

Le Château de ma mère follows the same principles. Pagnol describes his new life with Lili until it is threatened by the loom of school (pp.7-48). His plan to live as a hermit is thwarted (pp.49-96) and the autumn passes slowly (pp.97-111) but culminates in the Christmas holiday when Augustine hatches her plan for more regular visits (pp.112-30). Joseph is finally persuaded to take Bouzigue's key and the story of the 'four castles' begins (pp.131-69). After the brief interlude of Marcel's success in the scholarship exam (pp.170-73), the tale of the perilous short-cut moves through capture, fear and finally salvation (pp.174-213). A brief coda (pp.214-17) rounds off the volume with a mixture of fact and emotion. Thus the volume begins and ends on a documentary note: Lili introduces us to the flora and fauna and Pagnol speaks of the death of his loved ones and the purchase of La Buzine. The first term of Marcel's exam year is described impressionistically, while his failure to become a hermit and the longest section of the book, the story of the 'four castles', make exciting drama: they occupy almost a hundred pages and are strongly narrative in character. In quantitive terms, then, the balance seems to suggest that Pagnol's memories are nearer to fiction than to autobiography. It is an impression reinforced by well-marked structural parallels between the two novels: the same documentary, impressionistic and narrative elements are repeated and each volume ends on a note of high drama followed by a coda which draws a 'human' lesson from the tale that has been told.

But if the reader is left with an overall impression of experience made more interesting by art, the parts which make up the whole have an equally manufactured feel. The long episode which tells of Marcel's pursuit of the hunters and his role in his father's glory reads like an adventure which might have happened to the boy heroes of Twain or John Masefield. Even more artifice goes into the making of the story of the 'four castles', which is cunningly structured. After the members of the family make their first safe passage with Bouzigue, their unescorted forays into 'illegality' create a sense of danger which is dispelled in stages by the courtesy and warmth of the Count. They learn to feel safe in the grounds of the notary and, after an initial scare, Dominique makes them welcome in the third castle. Their fear of La Buzine maintains the suspense which, however, diminishes with custom and is forgotten when the scene changes to Marcel's examination ordeal. But their fear returns when they leave to spend the summer at Les Bellons, the last trial to face until their return which lies months away. Pagnol builds the suspense with practised ease (*Château*, p.174-83): Joseph does not sing as he shaves, Augustine has a 'pressentiment', they advance like frightened rabbits — and are caught. Creating and relaxing the tension at will, Pagnol teases the reader in his best story-telling manner. His tales are no less tall than the hunting stories of Jules which also work on the principle of 'et que vois-je?'

Pagnol, the practised raconteur, is quite unable to resist the temptation of writing up events and people as neatly shaped anecdotes. Jules's courtship of Rose, the visit to the 'brocanteur', the testing of Joseph's gun, the disagreement over Lamennais, the battle with the 'grosibou', Marcel's failure to become a hermit and others besides, are all detachable units. They have a beginning, a middle and an end and generally work upon the principle of ironic reversal: the tables are turned upon pride and pretension, so that Rose's prudish rechristening of Thomas as 'Jules' backfires on her and the 'manly' business of testing guns is deflated by the plaintive cry of the 'bonne'. No one is allowed to get away with anything. Joseph's glory goes to his head and his vanity is duly exposed to Marcel whose unquestioning faith in his father receives a rude jolt from which, however, he recovers. The caretaker of La Buzine bullies Joseph mercilessly but gets his comeuppance at the hands of Bouzigue. Marcel the free-thinking unbeliever is reduced to making the sign of the cross, and the future hermit who fears none of the wild creatures which exist in books is humbled by the thought of the wild boar which exist in reality: it is not he but Lili, slower but surer of foot, who comes off best. Pagnol's purpose may be that of an even-handed moralist who exposes self-importance and over-confidence, but he pursues it with relentless literary artifice. In narrative terms Pagnol rarely strays from the technique of the unexpected deflation. No self-image is sacred. Jules the master hunter is outperformed by his apprentice Joseph who is in turn overtaken by his pupil Bouzigue who is wiser in the ways of the world. Sometimes it is the reader who is taken down a peg. We warm to Paul's sensitive tears at the death of hunted creatures, but we are shaken by the immediate revelation that he would much rather torture his sister instead (*Château*, pp.32-33). Marcel acquires the habit of retailing his experiences not as unadorned statements but as 'de beaux récits'. There is every reason to believe that Pagnol never lost the habit of embellishment and that his tales are no less 'intéressants', 'pathétiques' and polished than those of his devious former self.

But they are also dramatic in an explicit theatrical sense. Pagnol's preface warns that he is a first-time 'writer of prose'. As a playwright, he had learned to avoid thrusting himself centre-stage and to express what he had to say through his characters and his handling of plot. Even the documentary preliminaries of *La Gloire de mon père* are heightened by touches of pure theatre: old André's obsession with the Pont du Gard is a small tragedy. And when Pagnol has no facts to relate about his birth, he has no compunction in turning the episode into a short domestic drama. At other times he needs no excuse: the incident of the 'bonne dans les cabinets' is a gem of farce. Nor is he able to prevent Marcel, who can adopt 'l'air formidable' at will, from playing a whole cast of parts, from Comanche to school genius. But as Pagnol warned Mme Lazareff, his forte was 'making people speak'. The proportion of dialogue to descriptive or reflective prose indicates how far Pagnol played to his strength. Joseph's dealing with the 'brocanteur' is so detailed and carefully written that a charge of imaginative fabrication would take little proving, and Bouzigue's account of how he dealt with the care-taker of La Buzine (*Château*, pp.206-09) even less.

But Pagnol was not merely a playwright but a film-maker too, and his visual imagination is everywhere apparent from the moment his ancestor explodes through the window of his workshop 'dans une apothéose d'étincelles' to the climax when Marcel brandishes 'la gloire de mon père en face du soleil couchant'. The epic battle waged with the 'grosibou' is as cinematographic as the tale of the 'four castles'. But Pagnol's film-maker's eye is detectable in smaller moments too: in the raindrops on the window pane which echo the sad tears on Marcel's cheek, or in the inkblot which closes his reply to Lili 'comme un soleil' (*Château*, pp.60, 111). Pagnol brings to the story of his childhood all his experience as a creator of spectacle.

In a real sense too, the characters he describes are first cousins to the characters which he created in his plays and films. The world of the *Souvenirs d'enfance* is almost as resolutely male as his fictional world which is stronger in fathers than mothers. Just as visible is Pagnol's talent for creating ripe eccentrics — from the touchy Escartefigue and the fastidious Monsieur Brun in the Marseilles 'trilogie' to most of the villagers of *L'Eau des collines* — which fill his childhood memories with comparably picturesque caricatures: the Corsican concierge warns Augustine that Marcel's brain will explode, Mlle Guimard has a small moustache and her nose wiggles when she talks, François is not on speaking terms with his brother and Mond des Parpaillouns never washes. But eccentricity does not merely lurk in the background. It looms large in the members of Marcel's immediate family: Rose and her obsession with Gas, Paul's bloodthirsty glee, Joseph's inveterate pedagogical habits and political dogma, Jules's tall stories, Lili's spelling... Pagnol brings to his childhood his practised love of generalised dottiness which is regularly reversed by sudden turnings of tables and flashes of wistfulness which create the funny-sad smile of amused complicity which makes him so human a writer. But certain characters have an even more direct relationship with other members of his fictional family. Jules bears a distinct resemblance to the characters played by Charpin in the films: he is rich like Panisse whose pomposity he shares. But Joseph is the clearest Pagnol archtetype.

Or rather he is two. To begin with, he is an embryonic Jean de Florette who also transports his family to the hills. Like Jean, he has a florid vocabulary which he uses to transform reality into what he has decided it will become. The broken furniture is rechristened 'la base d'un mobilier rustique... Mes plans sont faits, et je sais où je vais' (*Gloire*, p.66). He converts the long trek into a 'promenade hygiénique' and declares walking to be 'le plus sain de tous les sports' (*Gloire*, p.81, *Château*, p.148). He has the same total faith in weather statistics and he theorises about geology from books which give him an intellectual control of the world: if his tomatoes and leeks do not grow, it is because the drought has not obeyed the normal pattern (*Château*, p.55). For Jean, who shapes the future by doing sums on a piece of paper, the stakes are higher, but Joseph is no less of an 'enfant des villes'.

Secondly, he is also a 'prisonnier des écoles' (*Gloire*, p.126). As a teacher, he is omnipotent in his classroom where his ethical standards are unchallenged and problems can always be solved according to the rules of arithmetic. But he is ill-equipped to act in less clear-cut situations. Bouzigue's offer of the key forces him to choose between conflicting interests: the good of his family and his reluctance to break the law. His refusal to compromise brings him close to Topaze who refuses to alter the marks of his pupil even though his job depends on it. Just as Topaze agrees to act as Castel-Bénac's front man for 'honourable' reasons (to save Suzy, to improve the standard of spelling in commercial letters and so on), so Joseph finds an excuse. He salves his conscience by offering his unpaid, unofficial services to the Canal Company in return for the key: indeed, he views himself as a public benefactor who will save Marseilles from drought and disease. Topaze ultimately learns to change, but Joseph's experience teaches him nothing: the last we hear of him in *Le Château de ma mère* is his indignant protest that sinners patently prosper. We know that Marcel is the son of Joseph Pagnol (1869-1951), *instituteur*. And yet it seems no less clear that 'Joseph', who is clearly related to Jean de Florette and Topaze, is the offspring of Pagnol's imagination and therefore no less a member of his literary brood.

If Pagnol's characters have a family air which admirers of his films will easily recognise, his handling of them is equally familiar. He lets them have their heads before calling them to order on the principle that pride always comes before a fall — and the fall is usually caused by a metaphorical banana skin. Pagnol does not analyse their psychology but reveals it through actions, reactions, speech and gesture according to the requirements of theatre and cinema. The good-heartedness of Bouzigue emerges from the delicate way he persuades Joseph that he is a public benefactor. Under his 'chapeau d'artiste', the idiosyncratic dignity of the 'brocanteur' appears clearly long before Pagnol sums him up for us as a 'généreux vieillard'.

Both as playwright and cinéaste, Pagnol had acquired a way with character which conforms to the laws of realistic drama. But as a 'prose-writer', he was faced with a new problem: how to find words to convey what stage sets and camera show but do not describe.

Some of his physical descriptions of his characters are no more detailed than the stage directions in his plays. In *Marius*, Panisse 'a cinquante-quatre ans. Taille moyenne, ventre rond, moustache frisée au petit fer. Il a des espadrilles. Il est en bras de chemise et fume la pipe'. The 'brocanteur' is presented with comparable brevity: '[il] était très grand, très maigre, et très sale. Il portait une barbe grise, et des cheveux de troubadour sortaient d'un grand chapeau d'artiste. Son air était mélancolique, et il fumait une pipe en terre' (*Gloire*, p.61). Oncle Jules first appears thus: 'Sa figure était vieux rose; il avait une épaisse moustache châtain, des sourcils roux et bien fournis, de gros yeux bleus, un peu saillants. Sur ses tempes, quelques fils blancs' (*ib.*, p.39). Such sketches seem like no more than helpful hints for a casting director.

But Pagnol manages the description of settings much more satisfactorily. The story of Marcel's childhood unfolds against a background of well-documented reality. The thumb-nail sketches of people are accompanied by glimpses of the clothes they wear and echoes of the way they speak. He gives us an exact idea of the topography of the hills which change with storm, mist and winter. He says enough of the habits of country people to anchor them in general reality and gives a clear idea of particular objects, like the storm lantern. In other words, just as his concept of psychology draws on the tradition of the French *moralistes*, so his representation of physical reality is rooted in the conventions of realism.

Yet this realism is constantly undermined not merely by caricature and a marked taste for the eccentric but by a whole range of comic effects. Pagnol moves easily from the faintest hint of disparagement to the 'gros rire' of physical and even slapstick comedy. Often the humour derives from his temperamental taste for quirky observation, such as the Tati-like comment that the queue for the tram does not grow longer but denser, or the mixed metaphor he inserts into Bouzigue's declaration that 'cette clef va plus vite qu'une automobile' (*Château*, pp.117, 145). Bouzigue's boast is an instance of the *galéjade*, the fondness for exaggeration associated with the imagination of the 'gens du Midi', and Pagnol exploits this kind of verbal extravagance to the full. Marcel believes that Joseph has had 'bartavelles' dangling from his belt by the neck for so long that 'nous finirions par manger des cygnes' (*Gloire*, p.214). Lili's method of growing beans — plant them and run — is as succulent as his brother's juicy remark about people who cannot detect rain (*Château*, pp.202-03, 35). But Pagnol also plunders the repertoire of classical techniques. He consistently exploits the comedy of character by showing the distance which separates an individual's view of himself from reality — Joseph's 'gloire' being the prize example — but he combines it successfully with the comedy of situation based on the unexpected reversal. While his handling of such effects is subtle (as in the passing comment that Jules never contradicted Rose, especially when he was right), Pagnol is equally at home with a much cruder humour rooted in farce which runs from small details like the petomanic conclusion to François's 'savante explication' of the etymology of Taoumé and Tubé, or the table that falls on Joseph's head or the drunk removal man's 'éructation tonitruante' (*Gloire*, pp.88, 93, 95), to extended episodes such as Bouzigue's account of his sister and his victory over the caretaker of La Buzine. But if there is a single comic principle which underlies all others, it is Pagnol's wry, affectionate irony.

Pagnol ironises constantly. No member of the family escapes disparagement, for what they are and do is subjected to a constant barrage of gentle mockery. Ridicule is quietly poured all over old André's naïve belief in Education, Joseph's political and moral clichés and Jules's hunting bravado. No quarter is shown for Pagnol's younger self which is supremely vulnerable to romantic fancies, and not even Augustine is spared. She might cleverly rearrange Joseph's timetable, but she is scarcely 'le Génie de l'Intrigue', nor is Joseph a Great Hunter, although he brings off the 'coup du roi'. Even that great exploit is somewhat diminished by the low-key definition Pagnol later gives of 'gloire' which, far from the noble idea of heroic integrity suggested by Corneille's use of the word, has a banal meaning: 'la gloire, c'est quand on parle de vous' (*Amours*, p.43). Pagnol's ironical habits consistently point up the contradictions between words and actions: Augustine is sorry for little birds but thinks roast thrush is quite delicious, while the men's heated quarrels never diminish their friendship. But irony turns to satire when Pagnol undermines his family's social pretensions. Their basement turns into Joseph's 'atelier' and La Bastide Neuve (which has been 'new' for many years) becomes a 'villa' with a 'jardin' and a serving girl whom Jules calls the 'bonne'. Their transformation into 'bourgeois distingués' (*Gloire*, p.102) is further confirmed by the box containing a lump of ice which is dubbed a 'glacière' and by the family 'argenterie' which is tinplated (*Gloire*, p.203, *Château*, p.176). In all this, Pagnol mocks their vanity and self-importance and the 'small events' of which Marcel is a witness are regularly sent up by parody: the omnibus driver's hooter becomes an 'olifant' (*Château*, p.98) and by calling the hunting trip 'un épopée cygénétique' Pagnol gives it a ludicrous dignity which it never had — save, of course, to those who took part in it.

Pagnol's irony, then, takes a variety of classic forms — satire, parody, a general hyperbole — and is all-pervasive. Yet there is no hint of bitterness, for none of his criticisms are intended seriously. The sins of his family are small ones and they raise a smile rather than an eyebrow: their 'fault' is that they take themselves so seriously. Pagnol is never uncharitable and there is far less substance in the charges he makes than in the language with which he makes them. He consistently injects a sense of drama by labelling minor upsets 'catastrophes' and 'tragedies' or by calling a knife 'terrible', evoking a 'placard fatidique' and alluding evocatively to the 'impitoyables démentis' of the thermometer which refuses to make Marcel ill (*Château*, p.62). There is even more violence in words like 'étrangler' and 'foudroyer' which evoke the hunters' murderous intent than in most of the exploits we are shown. In the same inflationary vein, Marcel's reactions to what goes on around him and to him are limited in range. He may be 'terrorisé' and 'stupéfait', but we can see that he is no more than scared and surprised. His disappointment runs through a small scale of 'consterné', écoeuré', 'navré' and 'vexé', but none of his grief runs deep nor does it last longer than the occasional sense of shame or humiliation in minor matters. Of course, he does react 'avec feu' and often laughs 'aux larmes'; when pleased, he 'blushes with pride' and he saves face with the verb 'ricaner'. The constant repetition of such expressions serves to give a comic gloss to Marcel's simple emotions. In the absence of real drama (everyone is terribly good-natured), Pagnol consistently invests happenings with verbal drama and to some degree his *Souvenirs d'enfance* are a spoof on the grimmer kind of 'Childhood' as recounted by Gorki, say, or Jules Renard.

But what Pagnol's ironies also make clear is the degree of conscious control which he exerts over his memories. His voice is omnipresent and he keeps a firm hold on his tale through his mastery of language. When he addresses the reader directly, it is usually through general statements which have the form but not always the content of the well turned aphorism: 'la cigarette ne supporte pas la poudre', he says with mock sententiousness, and remarks in similar vein that 'les éboulis ont une tendance naturelle à s'ébouler'. Here the joke is on us. When he permits his characters to speak, the laugh is usually on them. What they say is as carefully judged to reveal their folly as the dialogue of any film or play he ever wrote. He occasionally reports their actual words, but the effect is not to strengthen the impression of realism. The quotation marks which indicate their 'authentic' voice usually point up the banality or absurdity of what is said: the curé's courtesy becomes all the more genuine because Joseph believes that 'ces gens profitent de tout' (*Gloire*, p.210). François is allowed to praise winter savory so that we can hear him say 'hacher finfinfin'; Paul says 'couillon', thus demonstrating that 'il avait déjà de la conversation' (*ib.*, p.89). All voices in the *Souvenirs d'enfance* belong to Pagnol who speaks with his tongue firmly in his cheek.

His linguistic control is nowhere more clearly signalled than in his use of inappropriately elevated vocabulary and over-elegant turns of style. Like Hitchcock, who as a film director never left anything to chance, Pagnol does not often allow us to draw our own conclusions for he guides us very firmly. The effects are most apparent in his reporting of events and conversations, such as his fastidious account of Marcel's letter to Lili (*Château*, pp.109-10), or Lili's description of 'la surprenante célérité du haricot hâtif' (*ib.*, p.202), or the richly ironic summary of the effects of alcohol on the average liver as pictured in classroom posters:

> On y voyait des foies rougeâtres et si parfaitement méconnaissables, à cause de leurs boursouflures vertes et de leurs étranglements violacés qui leur donnaient la forme d'un topinambour: mais pour éclairer ce désastre, l'artiste avait peint, au beau milieu du tableau, le foie appétissant du bon citoyen, dont la masse harmonieuse et le rouge triomphal permettaient de mesurer la gravité des catastrophes circonscrites. (*Gloire*, p.17)

Words as polysyllabic as possible are arranged in balancing groups leavened with visual surprises — the unexpected image of the knobbly Jerusalem artichoke or the word 'appetising' as applied to a healthy liver. As a rule, to increase the ponderous effect, Pagnol regularly places his sonorous adjectives in front of nouns in sentences which frequently appeal to the senses and culminate in an impressionistic or graphic image. The sound and movement of the departing tram are reinforced by three stages of a description which transports us, like Marcel, into a world of fantasy: 'Dans un brillant tintamarre de ferrailles, au tremblement cliquetant de ses vitres, et avec de longs cris aigus dans les courbes, le prodigieux véhicule s'élança vers l'avenir' (*Gloire*, p.76).

Pagnol's ironically overblown presentation of reality derives very largely from this choice and placing of adjectives which give an inflated importance to matters which do not normally receive such royal treatment. The tunnel diggers meet by accident after 'une longue et sinueuse flânerie souterraine' (*Château*, p.118). To prevent their possessions rattling in their packs, the spaces between are filled with 'sourdes châtaignes' and 'lingeries protectrices'. The chestnuts here are not, of course, noiseless, and 'sourdes' is one instance of the tranferred epithet which Pagnol uses extensively: 'la consolante crême fouettée' which pacifies Marcel, the 'roses tremblantes' which reveal Augustine's fear or 'le cliquetis coupable' of the wire which Joseph the 'criminal' uses to pick the lock at La Buzine, are other examples. Pagnol's mastery of language is fully exploited not simply to convey meaning but to give a carefully angled sight of reality. Pagnol's style works like a camera fitted with a filter which allows only certain kinds of light to pass.

But other stylistic techniques shape Pagnol's reality for us, and notable among them is the personification of nature. The circumstances of Marcel's birth are attended by favourable signs. As Augustine returns to Aubagne, 'la moitié d'un grand soleil rouge nous regardait à travers les pins' (*Gloire*, p.24), and for as long as Marcel assumes the external world was made for his amusement, nature remains friendly. Water 'sings', 'talks to itself' or weeps quietly 'dans une barbe de mousse'. Thyme plants 'étaient descendues à ma rencontre, pour annoncer au petit écolier le parfum futur de Virgile' (*ib.*, p.91). But as he observes more closely, he sees that nature is full of death as well as life: the 'impassive' flame of the lantern 'devours' insects which burn 'd'un impossible amour' (*ib.*, p.101). Velvet spiders dress up flies in silk and eat them 'avec un plaisir de gourmet'. Dormice perform a sarabande in the roof and the air over Taoumé 'dances' in the heat. When Marcel gets lost, nature treats him as she treats all living things. Paths he has travelled look quite different when he retraces his steps, for they become less friendly and 'en profitent pour changer de visage' (*ib.*, p.183). Marcel learns that Chantepierre alters its mood, for though it can sing sweetly, the mistral makes it angry and the rain-wind makes it anxious (*Château*, p.29). When he and Lili are fog-bound, the echo at Escauprés answers 'par pitié' and 'la pluie... comprit: elle s'arrêta' (*ib.*, p.48). But Marcel loses his privileged status. Summer passes without telling him, autumn sneaks up and drives him out and 'l'aggression subite de l'hiver' spares no living thing: 'les figuiers... n'avaient pas envie de parler'. Pagnol's use of personification allows him to chart Marcel's relationship with nature in graphic terms, for the natural world grows less attentive and less sympathetic as he grows older and becomes simply another of nature's creatures. It is one more lesson: nature goes her own way and he has no choice but to follow, a subject and no longer a prince.

A similar complicity between Marcel and his surroundings is suggested through a bold and highly visible use of imagery. Most of the time, Pagnol studs his sentences with simple similes and metaphors, but on occasions he develops extended images (the anticlerical *instituteurs* are the equivalent of 'missionaries' and belong to a 'church', he notes ironically, *Gloire*, p.20) while others (Marcel as an Indian) are strung together into a running joke. Metaphor is regularly used to express Pagnol's lyrical appreciation of nature: night is 'brodé de brumes blanches', the hills are 'fringed' with the red of dawn and the blossoming almond-trees are 'chargés de neige' (*Château*, pp.8, 94, 157). But a series of similes also shows children as part of nature. Paul is a toad, Lili a monkey, 'la petite soeur' a cat, while Marcel, who learns to read 'parrot-fashion', runs after Joseph and Jules 'léger comme une gerboise' before turning as he tires into a goat and then a calf. Jules is a bear, but Joseph is compared ironically to a bishop. For Augustine, Pagnol chooses images which reveal her fragility and his concern for her: she is a pretty Canadian skater but also a vulnerable sleep-walker standing on the edge of a roof (*ib.*, pp.116, 144). Even more striking, however, is the consistent way in which Pagnol uses imagery to show how Marcel tries to make sense of the new world of nature. Natural phenomena are translated into urban terms. The shoulders of Taoumé are like the folds of Mlle Guimard's coat, and the setting sun is like a picture on a sweet-tin (*Gloire*, pp.68, 195-96). The ants which Marcel and Paul burn march busily 'comme les dockers sur la passerelle d'un navire', bearing off the insides of the 'pregadiou' like Christmas shoppers (*Gloire*, pp.105, 108). Marcel visualises Jules's comment that a hare 'porte le coup de fusil' in terms of clothes and compares his feelings of excitement when inspecting a snare not only with that of a doughty trapper but also with the more mundane reaction of the lottery ticket-holder who waits for his number to be called (*Château*, pp.18, 26). But after Marcel returns to school, the process is reversed and the urban is described in terms of the countryside. Town is an 'ant-hill' and Marcel watches the minutes pass 'comme des fourmis décapitées' (*ib.*, pp.77, 105). This last example not only reveals that Marcel's heart is still in the hills but is also one of the highly visual and amusing images which are built on the principle of incongruity. The lizard's tail is left in the hand like the jacket of the thief pursued by a policeman, the mule's sides heave like a bellows in a bag, and Marcel's dictation passage is mined with traps like 'une plage de débarquement'. Marcel and Paul have legs like spaghetti, Dominique sports eyelashes like hairy anchovies and his dog is covered with bald patches 'qui ressemblaient à des cartes de géographie'. Pagnol had a facility for devising striking, graphic images which add considerable flavour to his stories. They are amusing and picturesque and they create a mood of sustained good humour.

On the other hand, they must also be seen as part of his overall battery of literary techniques which subvert the plain truth of his memories. Pagnol's skill as a writer is very evident in the way he fashions his narrative and reveals character in structured situations. His control of his material is total but is it a shade too professional? He turns his childhood into a kind of farce played out by eccentrics who are allowed to go only as far as their creator allows. His irony is so insistent that it begins to look increasingly like a defence mechanism designed to hide truths which he had no intention of revealing. Pagnol abandons his documentary interest in his past at an early stage of the proceedings and thereafter the realism if not the reality of the world he re-creates falters as though undermined by his refusal to delve into serious matters and by the sheer ease with which he directs our responses by means of his brilliantly subtle manipulations of language. His total mastery of the techniques of oblique representation through style — such splendidly consistent personification, such lush and cunningly contrived images — suggests that the *Souvenirs d'enfance* sacrifice truth, sobriety and honesty to art. Could it be that Pagnol is caught 'en flagrant délit de littérature'? Perhaps the measure of his literary artifice will be clearer if we examine how the same material is presented in a different medium: the versions of *La Gloire de mon père* and *Le Château de ma mère* directed by Yves Robert for the cinema in 1990.

5. 'Les Souvenirs d'enfance' in the cinema

Yves Robert first approached Pagnol for permission to film the books in 1963. He had made *La Guerre des boutons* (1961) and was known for his sensitive directing of children. Pagnol refused since he planned to film his autobiography himself (see above, pp.13-14). In 1972, Robert made another approach. This time, Pagnol did not say no but died before an agreement could be formalised. It was only in 1988, after the success of Claude Berri's versions of *Jean de Florette* and *Manon des sources*, that permission was given. Both films were made simultaneously on locations in Marseilles, the hills above Aubagne, and at Allauch. The village scenes were shot at Grambois, half way between Apt and Aix, since La Treille and its approaches had been changed beyond recognition by a century of urban sprawl. Filming took five months and consumed a budget of 90 million francs.

Although Pagnol's text abounds in cinematic moments (see above, p.66), turning his memories into a film script presented considerable difficulties. Pagnol's novel, *L'Eau des Collines*, provided Claude Berri with strong characters, an urgent tale to tell and a tragic outcome. In comparison, his autobiography is leisurely and diffuse and its big moments — Joseph's *coup du roi* and his discomfiture at the hands of a bully — are tremendous trifles and hardly strong enough to generate the tension needed to grip an audience. Moreover, no director could afford to take too many liberties with the text which is now known, it is estimated, to over three million readers. Pagnol, who has had over 150 schools named after him, is the most read author in France and, on the release of *La Gloire de mon père*, fifteen thousand copies of the book were being sold daily. For Yves Robert, the challenge was to heighten the drama without departing from the text.

The film of *La Gloire de mon père* dispenses with the documentary preliminaries. Instead, to establish Joseph's 'omniscience' in preparation for his subsequent lecturing and his arguments with Jules, Robert includes an extract from a speech delivered by Pagnol in 1962 at the inauguration of the Lycée Pagnol at Saint-Loup in which he recalled his father's faith in progress and his belief in science (for the text, see *Paris Match*, 20 October 1962). Joseph's devotion to his profession is neatly linked to Marcel's ability to read in a classroom sequence which looms larger in the film than in *La Gloire de mon père*, and a number of incidents are developed from what, in the original, are hints or passing references. Joseph's skill at *pétanque* is shown in a way not anticipated in the book and here and there Robert adds a few lines of dialogue or a small piece of business (Mastoc swallowing the key) which are new but generally in the spirit of Pagnol. However, an awkard note is occasionally struck: Joseph behaves unexpectedly badly to the *curé* at their first meeting and Lili steps out of character when he asks to keep the sailor suit which he has been given to replace his wet clothes. But with a few exceptions of this sort, little material foreign to the originals is included. Robert stays remarkably close the text and Pagnol's dialogues, suitably pruned, are retained throughout.

However, the order of certain episodes is changed. Joseph's tirades against capitalism are transferred to *Le Château de ma mère* where they are more appropriate. Monsieur Arnaud's vanity, instead of being a memory (*Gloire*, p.206), figures earlier in a lively scene intended to be a more elaborate preparation for Joseph's own later boasting. However, readers will note that Robert moves well beyond the bounds of both volumes. Marcel's friendship with Lili, which Pagnol reserved for his second volume, begins now with their chance meeting on the opening day of the hunting season: ninety pages of *Le Château de ma mère* (pp.11-101) are brought forward. Similarly, Marcel's enslavement by Isabelle is taken from the third volume of the series, *Le Temps des secrets* (pp.66-165), and inserted into the second film. The justification for both transpositions is that they strengthen the narrative and fill out the action. No harm is done by introducing Isabelle at an earlier stage and much is gained. But by promoting Lili, Robert disturbs the architecture of *La Gloire de mon père*. Pagnol made Marcel's new understanding of his father's humanity the high point of the first volume; in the film, the climax centres on his friendship with Lili. Thus Marcel's deepening under-standing of his father, central to the continuing story of their relationship, loses much of its impact. Indeed, *Le Château de ma mère* focuses more sharply on Joseph while Marcel is made to seem rather passive for long periods: he is reduced to looking on helplessly while his father commands our attention.

The sidelining of Marcel highlights the thorniest problem of adapting the books for the screen. Pagnol told his story from the inside, presenting events through Marcel's eyes and his own gentle irony: as a writer, he retains control for he directs our attention at what he wants us to see. Film, on the other hand, is best when it shows events and character in action. By externalising Pagnol's memories (as he must if we are to see them), Robert cannot avoid giving people and events an independent existence which enables them to escape Marcel's uncertain grasp of them. Paul is a much more definite character; Jules has a much more forceful and sympathetic presence, while Isabelle's tyranny emerges even more clearly for being visible. In other words, Robert creates a distance between Marcel and the world outside him, though Pagnol had made him the central 'witness' of events. The books are Marcel-centred: we see through his eye. The films make him much more of an observer of events which we see in much the same way as he does. The films give us incidents to look at. They are less able to show how Marcel misinterprets and transforms reality, a process which is crucial to Pagnol's purpose and narrative technique. The effect is cumulative and ensures that Marcel's imagination is significantly diminished.

Although he loses contact with the hunters on the opening day of the season, we see much less of his fears and spirited determina-tion. Indeed, our first sight of Lili demystifies his plight for it is evident that Marcel cannot have strayed as far from safety as he thinks. For Pagnol, the whole point was precisely Marcel's belief that he is totally lost in a literary landscape full of bookish dangers. Here, as in a number of his struggles with the puzzling world of reality, film proves much less successful in getting inside Marcel's mind. Instead, they show him as a social figure. We observe his relationship with his family, with Lili and Isabelle, and with the landscape, but we do so from the outside. At critical moments, we see him act whereas Pagnol insists on showing him reacting to the world which he slowly masters. A whole psychological dimension — where are the references to the cruelty of little boys? — is thus underplayed.

Of course, Robert could not be expected to show us everything. A certain amount of selective pruning was inevitable and on the whole it is sensitively managed. We may regret mildly the demotion of the magic 'brocanteur' to an eccentric walk-on part, or the absence of the photogenic ink-blot on the letter he writes to Lili, but these are details. It does not matter greatly that we do not feel Marcel's excitement when he stands next to the 'wattman', nor hear Jules tell the tale of 'les tripes de Malbousquet', nor see anything of Marcel's rival, Silva. Yet Pagnol made his drama out of the accumulation of such trifles and Robert's versions lose much in the telling.

That this is so has more to do with the difference between literature and cinema than anything else. Robert was obviously aware of the problem and to restore the essential bond between the storyteller and the story he tells, he allows a dark brown Pagnol sound-alike to comment, very much as in the books, on events as they unfold. Pagnol's voice, affable, ironic and self-disparaging, adding touches of humour or pathos to what Robert enables us to see, dominates the films. The mood is Pagnol's as are the comedy and the fey wisdom. The voice-over is to the films what rosemary and thyme are to Augustine's 'civet de lapin'. These are two very literary and extremely talkative films and this explains in no small measure why some reviewers considered them unsatisfying in cinema terms. It may also be one reason why they have proved less popular abroad than in France where *La Gloire de mon père* has sold more seats than *Cyrano de Bergerac*. No sub-titler could possibly compete with Pagnol, and when robbed of his voice, the films may well appear mawkish to many.

But if Robert retains as much of Pagnol's point of view as possible, he also remains true to another of Pagnol's aims, for he provides a much fuller 'témoignage d'une époque disparue' than emerges from the books. From Augustine's sewing machine and François's cart, from the ladies' hats and the splendid hunting outfits to the trams in the streets of Marseilles, the handsomely populated Parc Borély and the lovingly recreated village of La Treille, Marcel's world is revealed in all its solidity. The camera closes on to an inkwell and opens on to soaring landscapes which are not silent but alive with the whirr of cicadas and the screech of birds of prey. There are performances to match and Robert proves yet again how good a director of children he is. Marcel can be seen thinking, Paul twinkles wickedly and Isabelle is deliciously horrible. Yet, paradoxically, the more the film succeeds in bringing Marcel's world to life, the further it strays from Pagnol's concern to show how by conquering that world through experience he had lost it.

Both films, shown in France on staggered release in 1990 and in the UK a year later, received a mixed reception. 'Depuis *Jean de Florette*,' wrote the *Journal de Genève* (4 November 1990), 'les adaptations des romans [*sic*] de Marcel Pagnol sont devenues un genre en soi: naturalisme mimé, couleur locale provençale, scoutisme bucolique, ce genre oscille entre le feuilleton télévisé et la pub pour fromage aux herbes.' *Le Château de ma mère* is 'une fastidieuse série d'épisodes rébarbatifs et passéistes.' Other reviewers added that Robert compounds Pagnol's sentimentality and called his screen versions too scrubbed, too civilised, too bland. The women are overdressed, the sets too perfect and the interiors too upmarket for a poorly-paid *instituteur*. Yves Robert, conscious of the international market, clearly went for the Hollywood touch. Country life is romanticised, caricature replaces observation and Marcel and company can at times seem closer to American teenagers than to turn-of-the-century French children. The glossy music serves less to underscore the mood of the films than to internationalise their appeal. If the big storm scene is effective, other moments are mishandled. Jules and Rose dance in the rain in the Parc Borély, yet it is obvious that the rain is falling only in front of the camera. Or again, Robert opts for a long shot of Marcel as he hoists his father's glory in the setting sun. The result is to make him and his gesture seem small and in any case the scene looks as though it were filmed not at sunset but in a strong mid-afternoon glare. Sasha Moorshom (*The Independent*, 10 February 1990), considered the venture to be an exercise in false nostalgia and deplored its resolutely Mediterranean apology of hunting: here is a film experience which can hardly be called green.

Yet most film-critics, in spite of such reservations, confessed to falling under the spell. For Jacques Siclier (*Le Monde*, 31 August 1990), *La Gloire de mon père* succeeded in conveying Pagnol's world very clearly. 'Le film d'Yves Robert sent bien les salles d'école primaire, les réunions de famille autour d'un gâteau, le thym des garrigues. On y voit des gens modestes s'aimer, se chamailler, vivre au rythme de leur époque, de leur milieu. On entend le bruit des boules de pétanque, le ruissellement de la fontaine sur la place du village, le chant des cigales, les cris de la nature. Le film est senti-mental, ce qui, pour moi, est une grande qualité, comme cela en sera une pour le public qui va chercher là son Pagnol et va le trouver.'

Yet, in a sense, Robert's strengths are also his weakness. If Pagnol's documentary fervour fades early it is because he was less interested in historical reality than in Marcel's changing view of his small world. However real and touching the films seem, they further subvert Pagnol's truth by adding another level of artifice: that of the cinema. The films offer a valuable point of comparison but do not help us greatly to resolve our question: how true as an autobio-grapher is Pagnol?

6. Conclusion

However artful the autobiographer, he cannot depart from the what-has-been. His past is made of events, people and reactions which are fixed and cannot be changed. He is bound by the pre-formed structure of the tale he has to tell: he cannot invent as a novelist invents, though, since he cannot tell all, he does have the freedom to give the what-has-been a shape. We have heard Pagnol admit that 'il a fallu inconsciemment resserrer, condenser' (see above, p.20). How much he changed the past through his unconscious creative processes is, of course, impossible to tell. But Pagnol's literary artifice conflicts with what we expect of the honest autobiographer, for the skill of the storyteller who constructs neat tales undermines both truth and spontaneity. Pagnol's manipulation of plot, character and in particular of language acts like a defence mechanism which shelters private emotion from the public gaze.

His declared reasons for writing about his past are unhelpful. He implies that he had no choice: it was a natural development prompted by bright memories which emerged unbidden into his mind and made him curious about the boy he once was. But he clearly had no intention of writing an apologia or settling old scores, nor was he seriously concerned to paint a picture of a bygone age. But nor is it enough to say that he simply enjoyed rummaging through his memories, taking an artist's pleasure in giving them a public form. 'Marcel' clearly intrigued him and he relished the business of re-creating him. The *Souvenirs d'enfance* may be a 'pious' celebration of his family and only intermittently an evocation of 'une époque disparue', but they are more than a collection of jolly anecdotes. Pagnol covers the 'classic' issues of the development of the self and indeed what he gives us coincides with the prescription for the 'Childhood' suggested by Richard Coe (see above, pp.17-18).

Pagnol conveys the 'uniqueness' of childhood through a sense of wonder, and his recollections express the 'truth' about his early years, show how Marcel makes sense of life by imposing patterns on it, feature archetypal figures and experiences and convert a small world into a boundless universe which awaits discovery.

It is quite obvious too that he was fascinated by the behaviour of children for he makes considerable efforts to understand and reproduce their concept of the world. He makes much of their cruelty. Marcel laughs at the cyclists in the park, throws stones at the duck to kill it and, with Paul, proceeds to torment insects: 'Telle est la gentillesse des "petits anges" de huit ans' (*Gloire*, p.73). Pagnol's rueful acceptance of their natural savagery is many times indicated by his ironic conversion of their barbarity into 'nos études': the 'observation scientifique' of a battle to the death between two 'pregadious' constitutes 'un spectacle charmant', 'un divertissement si gracieusement enfantin' (*ib.*, p.106). Marcel and Paul believe that war is the only game worth playing (*ib.*, p.111) and concoct horrible methods of killing their enemies. An odd mixture of feeling and insensitivity leads the egocentric Marcel to protect his mother and his brother, and leads Paul to stick broken insects together with glue and to prefer torturing his sister to hunting. Children have little capacity for 'la vraie amitié' (such as that which binds Joseph and Jules): 'ils n'ont que des "copains" ou des complices, et changent d'amis en changeant d'école ou de classe, ou même de banc' (*Château*, p.125). They are given to sudden enthusiasms which they forget quickly. Their reason is undeveloped beyond a certain capacity for deviousness (Marcel quickly learns how to blackmail his parents by exploiting their weaknesses) and they feel everything intensely. When Marcel realises that he must return to Marseilles and school, Jules describes as a 'petite déception' what to Marcel is the end of his world — and he knows no other. For he lives a compartmentalised existence which, abolishing time, is rooted in the immediate present made infinite by an endless capacity for make-believe.

Pagnol, in unusually theoretical mood, explains the self-containment of children by the notion that they live not in the real world but in a parallel universe of their own. He explains the closed-world phenomenon of childhood with a slightly embarrassed nod in the direction of the subjective idealism of Johann Gottlieb Fichte (1762-1814). Of course, Pagnol, who never claimed to be a philosopher, simplifies Fichte's complex analysis of the working of the mind. The Ego affirms itself unconditionally, but in so doing necessarily posits a negative — an opposite which is not self, the Non-Ego. This activity of the Ego is the essence of its existence but consciousness of itself derives solely from its opposition to the Non-Ego, i.e., the external world of objects. In Pagnol's broad terms, from the standpoint of ordinary consciousness, what we call the world is merely a product of the Ego through, for, and in which it exists. Because, in other words, children are programmed never to question the obvious fact that they are the centre of a world which they have invented to respond to their bidding, they throw tantrums when they cannot control what goes on around them, feel no remorse for their actions and are generally unaware that other people, animals and 'pregadious' are sentient beings like themselves. 'Jusqu'à la triste puberté, le monde des enfants n'est pas le nôtre: ils possèdent le don merveilleux d'ubiquité' (*Château*, p.73). And what is true of boys applies equally to girls, as the selfish, tyrannical Isabelle of *Le Temps des secrets* suggests.

It is this 'other' world of childhood that Pagnol tries to capture. Occasionally he oversteps the mark and gives Marcel rather sophisticated thoughts. Marcel precociously classes Jules as a 'vieillard', imagines the diseased liver of the removal man and dismisses his parents' fetishistic rules about washing in the classic manner of Richmal Crompton's William Brown: these reactions are not Marcel's but are instances of Pagnol's grown-up romanticising. But if a few such moments strike a rather self-conscious note, Pagnol provides many vivid insights into Marcel's mentality. He recreates the wonder of childhood through recollected sensation: the park is a place with lawns which urge boys to play on them and attendants to prevent them from doing so (*Gloire*, p.38). Why does moonlight coming through a round hole lie flat on a table? Do birds sing in patois? Marcel is curious about reality but rarely surprised by it, for his multiple personas allow him to wander freely through its marvels.

Pagnol, conspiring with Marcel's flight into his secret world, heightens reality with small spurts of poetry. The 'prodigious' tram heads not for La Barrasse but for 'l'avenir' (*Gloire*, pp.75-76): what François drives is not a cart but 'le chariot de l'aventure et de l'espoir' and when it has delivered the furniture, 's'envola dans le passé' (*ib.*, p.98). Reality is thus inserted between future and past in an eternal present. The gate of La Buzine opens on to a fairyland, 'la perspective ensoleillée de l'immensité des grandes vacances' (*Château*, p.178). As Joseph nails down the boxes for the return journey, 'je vis bien qu'il clouait le cercueil des vacances' (*ib.*, p.60). Within weeks, Joseph's bartavelles 's'étaient envolées dans une légende' (*ib.*, p.9) and the autumn lapwings 'partaient vers d'autres vacances' (*ib.*, p.48). Marcel gets his first scent of true friendship as he stares into the fire and sees 's'envoler... un oiseau bleu à tête d'or' (*ib.*, p.125). The switch of mood from the mundane to the super-real world (which the reader recognises as Never-Never Land, Oz and Narnia) is frequently engineered by a verb of motion ('s'envoler' especially) linked to an abstract destination which is not of the adult world but a zone of sparkling possibilities which assumed any shape Marcel wanted: the lost realm of childhood.

But Marcel is not its only inhabitant. Paul and to some extent Lili are also at home there, as might be expected. But the adults too are touched by the magic, for almost all are children in one way or another. Old André 'riait d'un rien, comme les enfants' (*Gloire*, p.28). Augustine can sometimes look no more than fifteen. Jules and Joseph squabble like little boys and their mothering wives regularly find ways of distracting them. Dominique quickly turns into a playground conspirator and his game of pretence reveals that 'le peuple... a la générosité des enfants' (*Château*, p.166). Not surprisingly, this pious thought is pronounced by Joseph who has a schoolboy passion for collecting junk and a sense of juvenile fun to which Marcel immediately responds. In the real world, Joseph cannot compete and Bouzigue accordingly speaks to him 'sur le ton d'une grande personne qui parle à un enfant' (*ib.*, p.147). But even this does not exhaust the list of children, for we must surely add Pagnol himself.

Both author and hero of the tale, Pagnol uses a 'double register' which enables him to be both himself and Marcel. From the outset, his narrator's voice divides into a variety of personas — the literary artist, the ironic observer of human folly, the (fairly) respectful son of Joseph and Augustine. Yet he is far less objective than his literary control suggests, for he shares Marcel's sense of wonder. The story of his birth is not 'étonnante' in itself, but it becomes so when he tells us about the amazing (but fanciful) parallel between his career and that of the abbé Barthélémy. When he speaks of the death of his grandfather Lansot, he makes a point of remarking: 'je m'étonne d'être le si vieux petit-fils d'un grand jeune homme' (*Gloire*, p.28). He intrudes into Marcel's world through sensations which he experiences afresh. He recalls the pepper in sausage and the taste of 'le pain craquant... d'autrefois' (*Gloire*, p.80). He describes the storm lantern in lyrical terms: 'Cette amande scintillante éclaire encore mon enfance': in comparison, a real lighthouse seems unremarkable (*ib.*, p.101). Later, he rode in motor-cars, but never again experienced 'cet orgueil triomphal d'être un petit d'homme, vainqueur de l'espace et du temps' that he felt on the tram to La Barrasse (*ib.*, p.76). Pagnol's memories are punctuated with the surprise of rediscovering what Marcel had felt: words like 'prodigieux' and 'merveilleux' mark his excitement and genuine pleasure. There is even something distinctly fey and Pooh-Bearish about the way he shows Marcel wondering where the shepherd had found enough stones to build his hut: 'Je compris dans un éclair de génie qu'il les avait prises là où il n'en restait plus' (*ib.*, p.193).

To Pagnol, such flights of fancy are clearly preferable to the road which the growing Marcel is required to travel. Marcel's personality becomes more sharply defined as his hold on external reality — time, place, things and people — grows stronger. As he develops, his imagination weakens and his splendid isolation is undermined as he is increasingly forced to acknowledge the reality of other people who make demands on him and, whether he likes it or not, will require him to be a rational, moral and social being. His development is of course unstoppable. But Pagnol makes no secret that he regrets the erosion of the imagination, the loss of the capacity for wonder and not least the acquisition of language which allows us to master the world so completely that we lose it entirely. By the start of *Le Temps des secrets* (p.22), the magic of the holidays has been eaten away by routine and even hunting has lost its charms:

> L'expérience, la "précieuse" expérience avait désen-chanté mes collines et dépeuplé les noires pinèdes: plus de lion, plus d'ours grizzly, pas même un loup-cervier solitaire. Ils avaient tous réintégré les pages illustrées de mon *Histoire naturelle* et je savais qu'ils n'en sortiraient jamais plus.

Many writers have regretted the loss of innocence in similar terms. Wordsworth revered 'the blessed vision of the happy child' which dims as 'Shades of the prison house begin to close / Upon the grow-ing boy'. For Nerval, 'Les illusions tombent les unes après les autres, comme les écorces d'un fruit, et le fruit, c'est l'expérience' (*Sylvie*, chap. xiv). John Betjeman lamented the passing of the heightened sensibility of the years of discovery: 'Childhood is measured out by sounds and smells / And sights, before the dark of reason grows' (*Summoned by Bells*, 1960). In Marcel's world, there are no tragedies or bullies, but even a happy childhood does not survive 'precious' experience and the 'dark of reason'.

Pagnol does not chart the loss of Innocence in general but of his innocence in particular, and his delight is as obvious as that of Scrooge who, transported by the Ghost of Christmas Past to his old school, says that of course he knows where he is — 'I know this place! I was a boy here!' — as though that explained everything. Scrooge took wrong turnings and made himself miserable. Pagnol never strayed so far and yet he too regrets the deadening hand of time which withers everything it touches. Pagnol aspires to a world of play which becomes real again with what he remembers of Marcel. Adulthood destroys the magic which can, however, be recaptured through imagination. At one level, the sense of play is revealed in Pagnol's delight in eccentricity and quirkiness. But at a profounder level, it enables him to transcend reality. As a literary creator, Pagnol is less like a man who plays God than the boy who changes a knife into a machete. He is lord of a make-believe universe which he defines through language and manipulates through those unexpected reversals which control the destinies of others. Fate does not rule the lives of the characters of Pagnol's autobiography in the way in which it directs the lives of Jean de Florette or Manon des sources, for in his dream world what he says goes. But he is a particularly tolerant controller. He is protective towards all his characters and rescues them from their folly: they are the children who must not be told that life consists of 'Quelques joies, très vite effacées par d'inoubliables chagrins' (*Château*, p.215). He mocks the family belief in education which does not lead to the triumph of right as Joseph believes nor to wealth, as Augustine assumes. Pagnol may not admire Joseph's missionary spirit and his natural 'purity', but they are respected as ideals. With his adult eye, he judges. But he remains enough of a child to know what has been lost.

Yet Pagnol is fully aware of the difference between the vision of a perfect world and reality. His characters come to no harm in the book but Pagnol himself becomes a victim of the passage of time. No amount of imagination can alter the fact that Lili, Paul and Augustine die, and the final ironic, irreversible reversal is directed at Pagnol himself. He breaks down the 'Porte du Père Humilié' and exorcises one ghost. But the other remains forever beyond his reach: the shade of Augustine is 'pour jamais inconsolable' (*Château*, p.218). Having re-created life, Pagnol makes the final, unanswerable discovery that he has no power over death.

All Pagnol's literary artifice leads him to this point of sincere confession. As Richard Coe remarks: 'By and large, the greater the writer, the more intense is the experience of childhood re-created, and the greater the need, in consequence, to refashion it in terms of poetic, or permanent significance' (*4*, p.8). Pagnol's re-created childhood may not be intense in the way that unhappy 'Childhoods' often are. And it may be more artful than most. Yet the *Souvenirs d'enfance* are no less honest, true and vivid for being written by an author who uses all his literary skills to feel his way back to the wonder years. Pagnol as an artist has the child's gift of ubiquity, for he can be himself and Marcel. But unlike Marcel, he can never be more than a visitor in Eden, for 'precious experience' stands like a dragon at the gate and balefully reveals to him the corrupting knowledge of what he has lost.

Glossary

adessias (interject.) (i.e. Prov., *à-diéu-sias*, 'God be with you')
  - goodbye

agasse (n.f.) (Prov., *agasso*) - magpie

aïgo boulido (n.f.) - 'quelques gousses d'aïl bouillies dans de
  l'eau' (*Château*, p.128); a garlic soup

alude (n.f.) (Prov., *aludo*) - large flying ant

argéras, argélas (n.m.) (Prov., *argelas*) - 'genêts épineux'
  (*Château*, p.142); gorse

barre (n.f.) - 'à-pics de roches, que les Provençaux appellent des
  "barres"' (*Gloire*, p.82)

baouco (n.f.) (Prov., *bauco*) - 'herbe jaune et brune... On aurait dit
  du foin séché' (*Gloire*, p.91)

bastide (n.f.) (Prov., *bastido*) - country or farm house

bédouïde (n.f.) (Prov., *bedouïdo*) - 'un genre d'alouette' (*Château*,
  p.14)

cabridan (n.m.) (Prov., *cabrian*) - 'd'énormes guêpes' (*Gloire*, p.101);
  hornet

cade (n.m.) (Prov., *cade*) - juniper

cul-blanc (n.m.) (Prov., *cuou-blanc*) - 'que les Français appellent "motteux'" (*Château*, p.14); wheatear

darnaga (n.m.) (Prov., *darnagas*) - 'Les gens de la ville leur disent "bec croisé'" (*Château*, p.14); shrike

escagasser (vb.) (Prov., *escagassa*) - to crush, shatter

fada, fadade (adj.) (Prov., *fada*) - stupid, simple-minded

garrigue (n.f.) (Prov., *garrigo*, cf. pre-Latin *garric*, oak) - scrub, moorland

graffigner (vb.) (Prov., *grafigna*) - to scratch ('égratigner')

gratte-cul (n.m.) (cf. Prov., *grata*, to scratch) - 'la baie de l'églantier' (*Château*, p.33); dog-rose, briar

jas (n.m.) (Prov., *jas*, a shelter) - a small hut or cabin

limbert (n.m.) (Prov., *limbert*) - a lizard, usually green, 'd'un vert éclatant, semé sur les flancs de très petits points d'or, et, sur le dos, de lunules bleues, d'un bleu de pastel' (*Château*, p.15). Cf. 'une grande scolopendre couleur de miel' (*ib.*, p.27)

litorne (n.m.)- See *sayre*

messugue (n.f.) (Prov., *massugo*, *messugo*) - rock-rose, Stinking Hellebore. The same as *ciste*, 'que les Anglais appellent "la rose des roches" et les Provençaux la "messugue'" (*Manon des sources*, éd. Fortunio, p.286)

parpailloun (n.m.) (Prov., *parpailloun*) - butterfly; Mond des Parpaillouns = Edmond des Papillons (*Gloire.*, p.130)

pèbre d'aï (n.m.) (Prov., *pebre d'ai*) - 'comme une espèce de thym, et en même temps une espèce de menthe' (*Gloire*, p.92); savory

pétélin (n.m.) (Prov., *petelin*) - French 'térébinthe': terebinth,
    turpentine tree

pétoulié (n.m.) (Prov., *petoulié*) - 'une nappe de crottes' (*Château*,
    p.14)

pitchounet (dimin. adj., from Prov., *pichot*, *pitchoun*, small) - 'Bravo,
    Pitchounet, me dit Mond' (*Gloire*, p.208)

pregadiou (n.m.) (Prov., *prégo-Diéu*) - praying mantis

rascasse (n.f.) (Prov., *rascasso*) - hog-fish

sayre (n.f) (cf.Prov., *cero*) - 'la grande grive des Alpes, celle que
    mon père avait un jour appelée "litorne"' (*Château*, p.66); a
    type of thrush

taravelle (n.f.) (Prov., *taravello*) - 'le rondin de bois dur qui est
    l'unique rayon du treuil de la charrette' (*Gloire*, p.97)

Bibliography

A. WORKS BY MARCEL PAGNOL

The four volumes of Pagnol's *Souvenirs d'enfance*, in chronological order are: *La Gloire de mon père* (1957), *Le Château de ma mère* (1958), *Le Temps des secrets* (1960) and *Le Temps des amours* (1977). They were first published by Les Editions de Provence but have all been issued in paperback form under a variety of imprints: Livre de Poche (to 1976), Presses-Pocket (to 1988) and currently Fortunio (Editions de Fallois) which are those referred to in the text. The first two volumes were translated by Rita Barisse as *The Days were Too Short* (New York, Doubleday; London, Hamish Hamilton, 1960; reprinted 1962 and London, André Deutsch, 1991). Rita Barisse also translated *The Time of Secrets* (London, Hamish Hamilton, 1962) and Eileen Ellenbogen the last of the quartet as *The Time of Love* (London, Hamish Hamilton, 1979): both were reissued in a single volume by André Deutsch in 1991.

The editions of *La Gloire de mon père* (1962) and *Le Château de ma mère* (1964) prepared by Joseph Marks for Harrap (now Nelson) have helpful glossaries and notes.

Pagnol's *Œuvres complètes* were issued by 'Le Club de l'Honnête Homme' in 12 volumes (1970-71).

B. PROBLEMS OF AUTOBIOGRAPHY

1. Philippe Lejeune, *L'Autobiographie en France*, Paris, A. Colin, 1971
2. ——, *Le Pacte autobiographique*, Paris, Seuil, 1975
3. Georges May, *L'Autobiographie*, Paris, P.U.F, 1979
4. Richard N. Coe, *When the Grass was Taller*, New Haven and London, Yale U.P., 1984
5. Bruno Vercier, 'Le mythe du premier souvenir', in *Revue de l'histoire littéraire de la France*, LXXV (1975), 1029-40

C. CRITICAL STUDIES

6. Gabriel d'Aubarède, 'Un débutant nommé Pagnol', in *Les Nouvelles littéraires* (16 May 1963), 1, 7
7. Georges Berni, *Merveilleux Pagnol*, Monte-Carlo, Editions Pastorelly, 1981
8. C.E.J. Caldicott, *Marcel Pagnol*, Boston, Twayne, 1977
9. Raymond Castans, *Marcel Pagnol m'a raconté...*, Paris, Editions de Provence / Editions de la Table Ronde, 1975; Folio, 1976
10. ——, *Il était une fois... Marcel Pagnol*, Paris, Julliard, 1978
11. ——, *Marcel Pagnol. Biographie*, Paris, Lattès, 1987; repr. Paris, Livre de Poche, 1988
12. David Coward, *L'Eau des collines: 'Jean de Florette', 'Manon des sources'*, Glasgow, 1990 (Glasgow Introductory Guides to French Literature, 9)
13. Marcel Mithois, 'Interview', in *Biblio*, XXXII, 3 (mars 1964), 7-9
14. Marcel Pagnol, *Topaze*, edited with an introduction by David Coward, London, Harrap, 1981
15. Nicole Pakenham, *La Gloire de mon père*, Exeter Tapes Series, no. F 7569.

D. FILMOGRAPHY

La Gloire de mon pére (My Father's Glory) (1990). Joseph (Philippe Caubère), Augustine (Nathalie Roussel), Jules (Didier Pain), Rose (Thérèse Liotard), Marcel à 5 ans (Benoît Martin), Marcel à 11 ans (Julien Ciamaca), Marcel's voice (Jean-Pierre Darras), Paul (Victorien Delemare), Lili des Bellons (Joris Molinas), Mond des Parpaillouns (Paul Crauchet), François (Pierre Maguelon).
Adapted by Jerôme Tonnerre, Louis Nucera and Yves Robert. Music by Vladimir Cosma. Photography by Robert Alazraki. Produced by Alain Poiré. Directed by Yves Robert. A co-production with Gaumont — Gaumont Production — Productions de la Gueville - TF1 Film Production, with the participation of the Centre National de la Cinématographie. Running time: 105 mins.

Le Château de ma mere (My Mother's Castle) (1990). Joseph (Philippe Caubère), Augustine (Nathalie Roussel), Jules (Didier Pain), Rose (Thérèse Liotard), Marcel à 11 ans (Julien Ciamaca), Marcel's voice (Jean-Pierre Darras), Marcel à 40 ans (Alain Ganas), Paul (Victorien Delemare), Lili des Bellons (Joris Molinas), Mond des Parpaillouns (Paul Crauchet), François (Pierre Maguelon), Isabelle (Julie Timmerman), Loïs de Montmajour (Jean

Rochefort), Le Comte (Georges Wilson), Bouzigue (Philippe Uchan), Vladimir (Ivan Romeuf).

Adapted by Jerôme Tonnerre and Yves Robert. Music by Vladimir Cosma. Photography by Robert Alazraki. Produced by Alain Poiré. Directed by Yves Robert. A co-production with Gaumont — Gaumont Production — Productions de la Gueville - TF1 Film Production, with the participation of the Centre National de la Cinématographie. Running time: 105 mins.

Both titles have a U certificate and were released in the UK on video on the Palace Classics label in 1991.

CRITICAL GUIDES TO FRENCH TEXTS

edited by

Roger Little, Wolfgang van Emden, David Williams